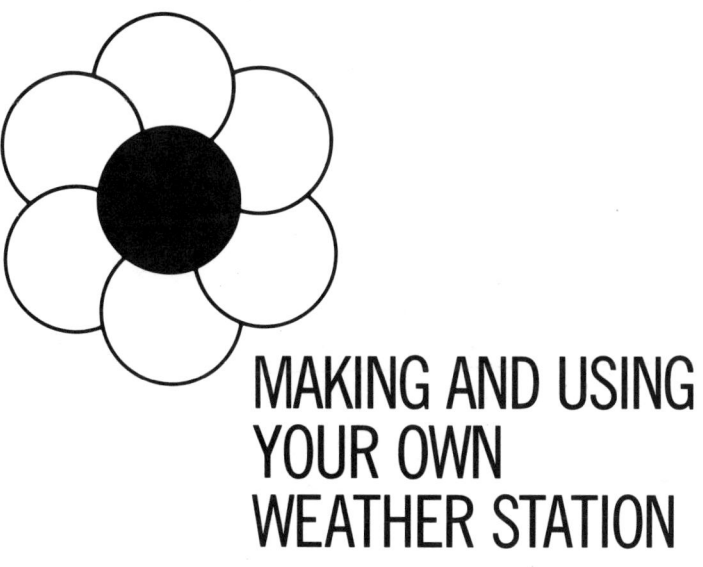

MAKING AND USING YOUR OWN WEATHER STATION

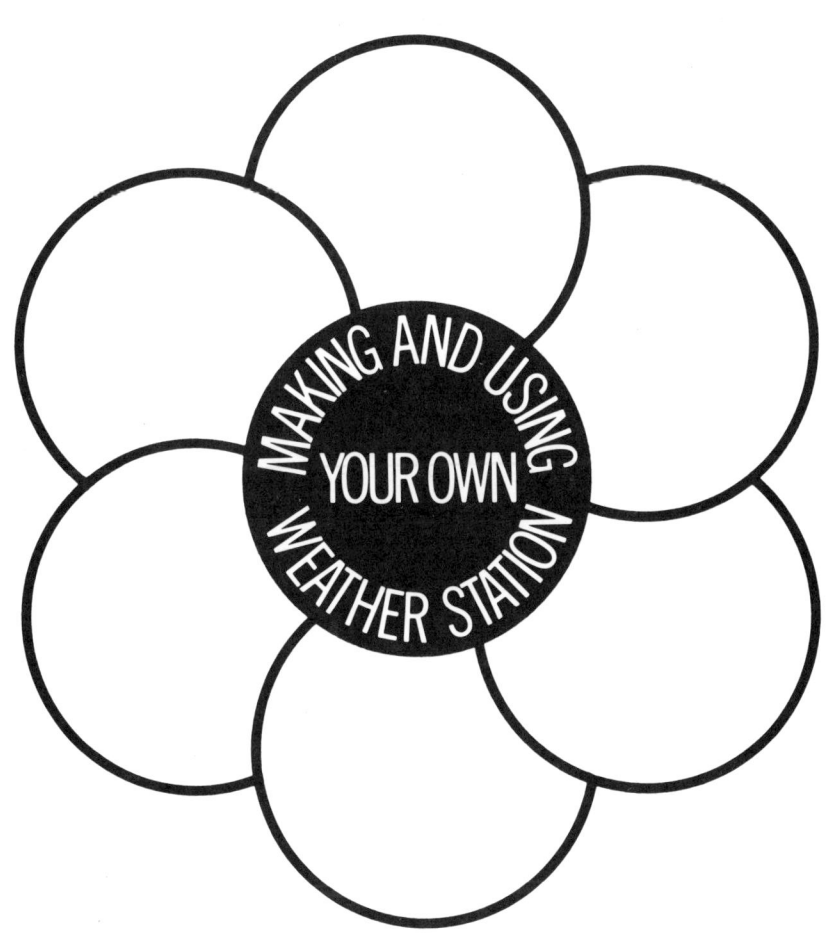

MAKING AND USING YOUR OWN WEATHER STATION

BY BEULAH TANNENBAUM
AND HAROLD E. TANNENBAUM

ILLUSTRATIONS BY ANNE CANEVARI GREEN
FRANKLIN WATTS 1989
NEW YORK   LONDON   TORONTO   SYDNEY
A VENTURE BOOK

Photographs courtesy of: AP/Wide World: p. 8; Voyager Aircraft, Inc.: p. 11; Bettmann Archive: pp. 14, 23; Granger Collection: pp. 36, 37; Edmund Scientific Co.: p. 48; Photo Researchers: pp. 56 (Spencer Grant), 57 (Kent & Donna Dannen), 63 (Russ Kinne); NOAA: pp. 71 (both), 72, 79, 82, 86, 96; Taurus: p. 85; Hughes Aircraft Co.: p. 94; New York Times: p. 98.

Library of Congress Cataloging-in-Publication Data
Tannenbaum, Beulah.
Making and using your own weather station / by Beulah Tannenbaum and Harold E. Tannenbaum ; illustrations by Anne Canevari Green.
  p. cm.—(A Venture book)
Bibliography: p.
Includes index.
Summary: Gives instructions for constructing simple weather instruments and how to use them to predict and record the weather.
  ISBN 0-531-10675-6
  1. Weather—Juvenile literature. 2. Meteorology—Experiments—Juvenile literature. 3. Weather forecasting—Juvenile literature. [1. Weather. 2. Meteorology—Experiments. 3. Weather forecasting. 4. Experiments.]
I. Tannenbaum, Harold E. II. Green, Anne Canevari, ill. III. Title.
QC981.3.T36 1989
551.6'3–dc19   88-31374 CIP AC

Copyright © 1989 by Beulah Tannenbaum and Harold E. Tannenbaum
All rights reserved
Printed in the United States of America
6 5 4 3

CONTENTS

CHAPTER ONE
Weather Around the World 9

CHAPTER TWO
Air Is Real *18*

CHAPTER THREE
Hot Air, Cold Air *32*

CHAPTER FOUR
Moisture in the Air *44*

CHAPTER FIVE
Winds and Clouds *55*

CHAPTER SIX
Storms 75

CHAPTER SEVEN
Recording and Predicting the Weather 91

Weather Instrument Suppliers 104

Glossary 105

Bibliography 107

Index 109

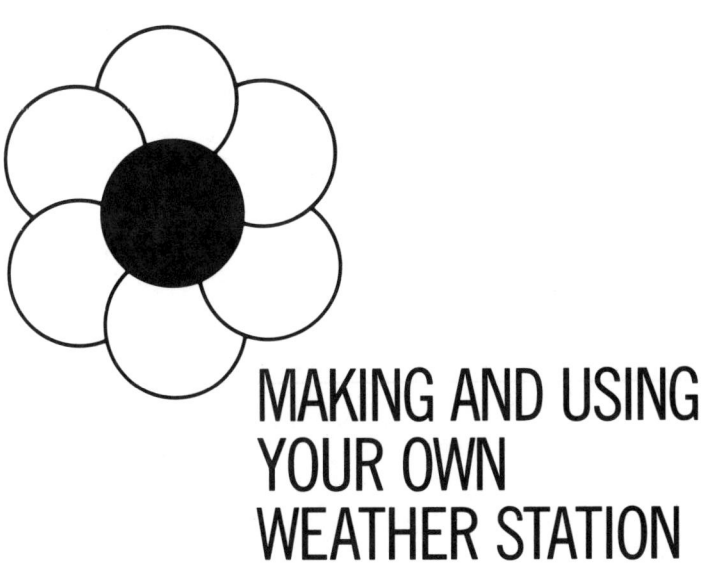

MAKING AND USING YOUR OWN WEATHER STATION

The experimental aircraft *Voyager* flew nonstop for eight days without refueling.

WEATHER AROUND THE WORLD

Just before Christmas 1986, *Voyager*, a weird-looking plane made of paper and plastic, landed in the Mohave Desert in California. It had taken off eight days earlier on a nonstop flight around the world without refueling. Even though the plane was built light so that it could carry plenty of fuel, the pilot insisted that a weather radar instrument be included. He won his argument because, as he said, from years of experience as a pilot, "I had acquired a healthy fear of weather." All the time the plane was in the air, *meteorologists* (weather scientists) were tracking it and providing it with additional weather information. The meteorologists, who had access to global weather reports and forecasts, could guide *Voyager* to skirt Typhoon Marge in the Pacific Ocean and to avoid several violent storms over central Africa.

Most daily uses of weather information are less dramatic than *Voyager*'s flight but are important for safety and comfort. Often, the takeoffs or landings of commercial aircraft have to be postponed because of weather conditions. Newspapers feature pictures of travelers stranded in airports waiting for the weather to change. And the launchings and landings of space vehicles frequently are held up because of "bad" weather. Weather reports are vital to land travelers also. Flood warnings allow drivers to avoid low-lying roads and unsafe bridges. Snow, sleet, and ice forecasts alert road crews to the possible need for plowing and sanding.

People constantly rely on weather forecasts in their daily activities and ask such questions as: "Should I take an umbrella?" "Do I need a coat?" "Should I close the windows before leaving the house?" "Can I take the boat out today?" "Can I go skiing?" "Do we have to cancel the game?" Farmers or gardeners who want to begin planting want to know when the last frost is expected. Also, they need to know the date of the first frost in the fall so that they can pick the remaining vegetables or bring the potted plants indoors. The frost dates depend on climate as well as on daily weather.

Meteorologists helped guide *Voyager* through several instances of violent weather on its trip.

Weather is the condition of the atmosphere for short periods of time: for an hour or for a day. *Climate* is the average weather for an area. For example, in Florida, the climate—the average weather—for December and January is frost-free. But occasionally the weather becomes very cold and a frost alert is posted so that the farmers can protect their orange trees when the temperature of the air is expected to fall below freezing—below 32°F (0°C).

Since the earliest times, people have been aware of the effects of the change in seasons. To prepare for winter, they knew they had to gather and store sufficient food to feed themselves until the next harvest. They knew when they had to leave their hunting grounds in the mountains and come down into the valleys to set up safe winter camps before the snows came. They knew more or less what the weather would be like each month, but they did not know what would happen tomorrow or the next day. Not until the middle of the eighteenth century were daily weather forecasts made.

People have always reported or recorded the weather. It was often the first item in a diary entry: "It rained all day" or "Today the weather changed; it turned cold." But without measuring devices, they could not report how much rain fell or what the temperature was. And not until 1743 did they have any sound basis for predicting weather. In that year, in Philadelphia, Benjamin Franklin planned to observe an eclipse of the moon which was to take place at 9 P.M. But by eight o'clock, clouds rolled in and a fierce northeaster—a storm with winds blowing from the northeast—raged all night and all the next day.

Franklin would have forgotten about the storm had he not read in a Boston newspaper an account of the eclipse describing the perfect viewing conditions. This surprised Franklin because he thought that since the winds blew from the northeast, the storm had come from that direction and that Boston would have had overcast skies even before 8 P.M. A letter from his brother, who lived in Boston, informed him that the eclipse was over an hour before the storm began. It occurred to Franklin that the path of these storms was not from the northeast but from the southwest.

To prove his theory, he questioned travelers arriving in Philadelphia from the south about the weather they had experienced. He also checked the weather conditions in Maryland, Virginia, and South Carolina as reported in local newspapers and in letters from friends in those colonies. His conclusion was that indeed such storms came from the south, originating over the "Bay (Gulf) of Mexico." And furthermore, if he knew what was happening in the south, he could predict the following day's weather for Philadelphia.

In a similar way, in 1783, a Polish scientist named Brande tracked the weather pattern across Europe. The main drawback to this first crude method of forecasting weather was that often by the time a weather report arrived from a distant city, the storm may already have reached and passed over the would-be

forecaster. Meteorologists had to wait about one hundred years until telegraphy became common enough to permit weather reports to be sent by wire from city to city.

Besides discovering where the storms originated, Franklin developed a theory of how storms from the "Bay of Mexico" were created. He did this by drawing on his knowledge of the basic work of earlier scientists: Evangelista Torricelli had proved that air has weight, Robert Boyle had shown that air could be compressed (squeezed into a smaller space), and Isaac Newton had established the three laws of motion. In his studies, Franklin also could use the thermometer improved by Gabriel Fahrenheit and the mercury barometer invented by Torricelli.

You too can be a meteorologist. You can make six weather instruments from the plans given in this book. You will be able to assemble your own weather station piece by piece with the instruments you make. You will also learn how to use the instruments to study, record, and predict the weather. Each instrument is described in the chapter in which the science related to it is presented. The instruments are easy to build, but if you prefer, you can purchase inexpensive commercial ones.

Ben Franklin performed many experiments related to the weather.

You can go through the book chapter by chapter and assemble one piece of equipment at a time. Or you can build or buy all the instruments at once, and then go through the book, performing the experiments and doing the projects. For those readers who wish to assemble the instruments in advance, the list below gives the page numbers where the directions can be found.

Instrument	Page
Barometer	20–29
Thermometer	38–40
Sling psychrometer	50
Rain gauge; snow gauge	52
Wind vane	60–64
Anemometer	65–69

Your weather station instruments may be crude compared to the automated, high-tech instruments used by the National Weather Service and by other professional meteorologists. Nevertheless, even without satellite data and computer analyses, you will be able to keep accurate local records and make simple short-term forecasts. A sample recording sheet is shown on page 101.

Your weather station need not have an elaborate outdoor structure. But for convenience in observing, all the instruments should be close together. You can mount each instrument separately or put up a small, sturdy platform to hold all the instruments. Suggestions for setting up your home weather station are given in Chapter Seven.

At the end of each chapter there are suggested activities for using the science information and instruments presented. You may wish to adapt some of these activities for classroom demonstrations or science fairs.

AIR IS REAL

No one knows when people first began to be concerned with the air around them, but early on they knew that air was there. Today, we use the term "air" interchangeably with "atmosphere". *Atmosphere* is a combination of two Greek words: *atmos*, meaning "vapor" or "gas," and *sphera*, meaning "sphere." The Greeks believed that the earth was a sphere surrounded by vapor. Early Greek scientists divided their environment into four "elements": fire, water, earth, and air. Some Greeks, like Anaximenes, who lived about twenty-five hundred years ago, believed that air was the basic element and that it could be compressed into water and further compressed into earth. Regardless of how they described air, they knew it was real.

Put your hand a few inches in front of your mouth and blow. What you feel is air pushing against your hand. Even though you cannot see air, even though it is invisible, air takes up space. When you swing your arm, when you walk, you push air aside. You can move air from one place to another. Use an unopened—flat—plastic or paper bag. Open the mouth of the bag and let air in; carry the bag across the room and then flatten it by squeezing the air out. You have moved the air that was in the bag from one place to another.

You can see that air takes up space. Fill a bowl with water. Hold a glass over the bowl with its mouth down. Slowly lower the glass straight down into the water. What happens? The water cannot rise in the glass because the glass is filled with air. Now, tilt the glass slightly and let the air pour out. Watch the air bubbles rise to the surface and the water fill the glass.

AIR PRESSURE • You can test the pressure (push) of air on an object. Fill a glass to the brim with tap water. Working over the sink, place a card over the mouth of the glass. Be sure there is no air (space) left between the card and the water. Turn the glass upside down. Why doesn't the card fall off and the water spill into the sink? Something must be pushing against the card, keeping it in place. That something is air, and it is pushing up against the card with a greater force than the force with which gravity is pulling the card and the water in the glass down.

Sometimes the air around us pushes more than at other times; we call this a change in *atmospheric pressure*, or air pressure. For more than three hundred years, people have known that when there is a change in atmospheric pressure, there is also a change in the weather. You can see what happens when air pressure is increased or decreased. Use a clear-plastic 1-pint (0.47 l) container with a tight-fitting clear-plastic cover. You will also need a glass tube or rigid clear-plastic tube ½ to ¾ inch (1 to 2 cm) in diameter and about 2½ inches (6 cm) longer than the height of the container, and a cork which will fit tightly into one end. An ordinary drinking straw completes the equipment. Refer to Figure 1.

1. Punch two holes in the cover so that the tube fits snugly into one and the straw into the other. You may need to line the holes with modeling clay or putty to ensure tight fits.

2. Fill the container about three-fourths of the way with water. Put on the cover.

3. Insert the tube into its hole and push it all the way down so that water rises in it. Fit the cork into the top of the tube to seal it.

4. Raise the tube slowly until the level of the water in the tube is about 3/4 inch (2 cm) above the container. Use a crayon to mark the level of the water in the tube.

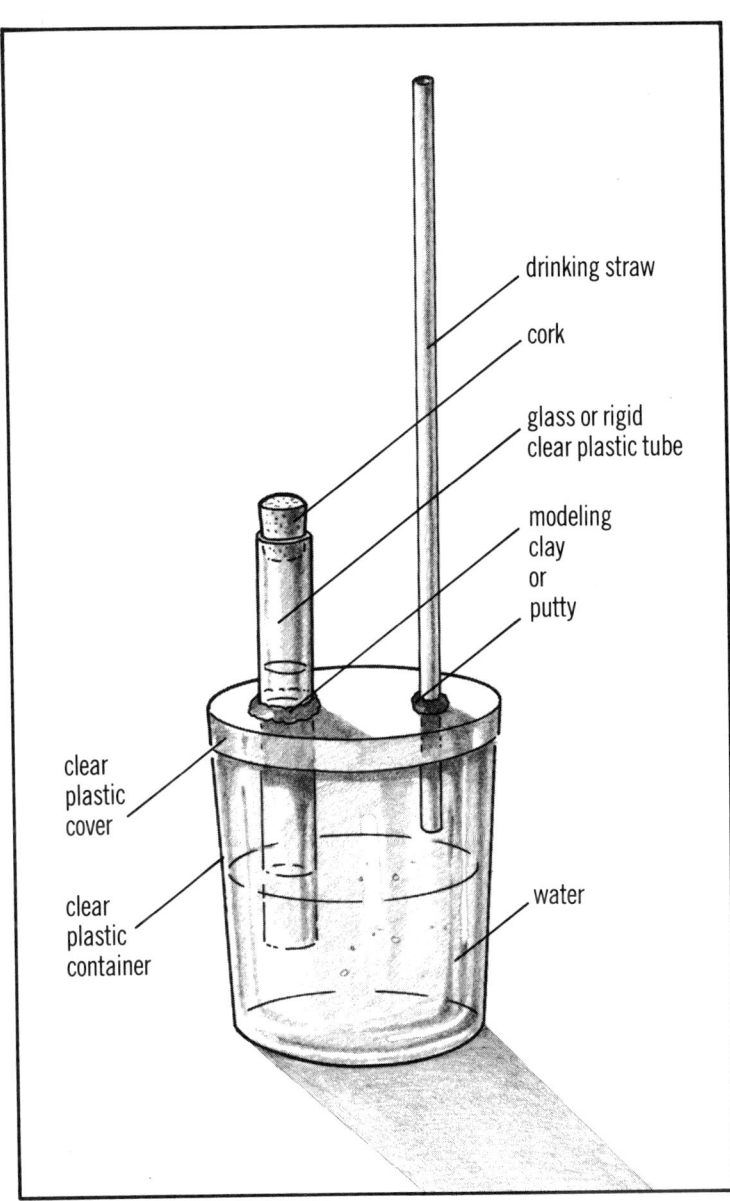

Figure 1. Setup for investigating air pressure

5. Insert the straw into the other hole, but do not let it reach the water.

Now you are ready to experiment with air pressure. Blow into the straw. What happens to the level of the water in the tube? Suck on the straw. Now, what happens to the level of the water in the tube? Before you used the straw, the air pressure in the container was "normal"; it could support a column of water as high as the crayon mark. When you blew into the straw, you increased the air pressure in the container and it could support a column of water higher than the crayon mark. When you sucked on the straw, you decreased the air pressure in the container and the water level fell.

BAROMETERS • Ordinarily, the atmospheric pressure can support a column of water 400 inches (1,000 cm) high. If you had a tube 440 inches (1,100 cm) long sealed at one end, you could fill it with water and then invert it into a tank of water. The excess water would flow out into the tank until the atmospheric pressure (the weight of a column of air) balanced the weight of the column of water. If the atmospheric pressure increased, the weight of the air could support more water and the column of water would rise. If the atmospheric pressure decreased, the weight of the air could support less water and the column of water would fall. Such an instrument which can measure air pressure is called a *barometer*. The name "barometer" is a combination of two Greek words: *baros*, meaning "heaviness" or "weight," and *me-*

tron, "to measure"; it measures the weight (pressure) of the air.

A 440-inch-tall instrument is clumsy. Perhaps some other liquid could be substituted for water (but not oil or alcohol, since they weigh less). In 1643, Evangelista Torricelli, an Italian scientist studying air pressure, decided to try liquid mercury, a silvery-white metal more than thirteen times as heavy as water.

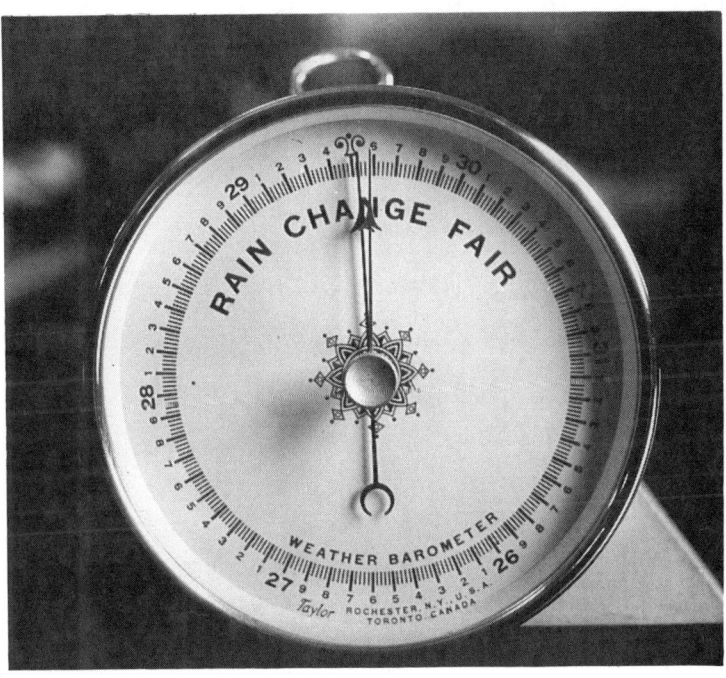

Barometers measure the air pressure.
High pressure means fair weather;
low pressure signifies stormy weather.

Torricelli used a tube a little more than 40 inches (1 m) long and sealed at one end. He filled the tube with mercury and held his thumb over the open end. Then he inverted the tube into a small tank of mercury. The mercury began to flow out of the tube, but not all of it; 29.9 inches (76.2 cm) remained, supported by the weight of the air pressing down on the mercury in the tank. While working on his air pressure experiment, Torricelli noticed that the height of the column of mercury was not constant; the weight of the air varied from time to time.

Torricelli had unintentionally made the first mercury barometer, the kind that was used exclusively for two hundred years to record air pressure and predict changes in the weather. The long glass tube and the partially open reservoir of mercury were often placed in fancy mountings. The old expression "the glass is falling" means that the barometric pressure is dropping. Torricelli's barometer worked because it was sensitive to the air pressure on the surface of the mercury in the reservoir. When he filled the tube with mercury, he forced the air out of the tube just as you did when you tilted the glass to let in the water. By inverting the tube in the reservoir of mercury, he let some of the mercury flow out but did not let in any air. He created an almost empty space—a *vacuum*—above the column of mercury. Then, only the pressure of the air outside was causing the change in the height of the column.

A mercury barometer, even a homemade one, can be *calibrated* (marked with inch or centimeter divisions) to give a true reading of air pressure. There is only one problem: *mercury is poisonous*! So, now we use another kind of barometer without either mercury or water. We call it an *aneroid* barometer; aneroid means "without liquid."

BUILDING AN ANEROID BAROMETER • In 1843, a French scientist, Lucien Vidie, wanted to make a small, portable barometer. He realized the importance of the vacuum in Torricelli's instrument, so he used an airtight can from which most of the air had been removed. He had a partial vacuum inside the can. Now, the outside of the can was sensitive to changes in atmospheric pressure. Vidie attached a needle to the can. When changes in atmospheric pressure caused the top of the can to move up or down, the needle moved with it. By placing a scale, marked in centimeters, behind the needle, he could measure the amount of pressure easily. The scale he made was based on the height of mercury in a Torricelli barometer.

You can make a demonstration aneroid barometer. Refer to Figure 2. You will need:

arts and crafts glue or household cement
a pint jar
a piece of rubber from a balloon, large enough to cover the mouth of the jar
3 rubber bands
a thin piece of balsa wood, about ½ inch (1 cm) wide and 1 inch (2.5 cm) high, with a wedge cut out of the top
a thin piece of balsa wood, about 1 inch (2.5 cm)

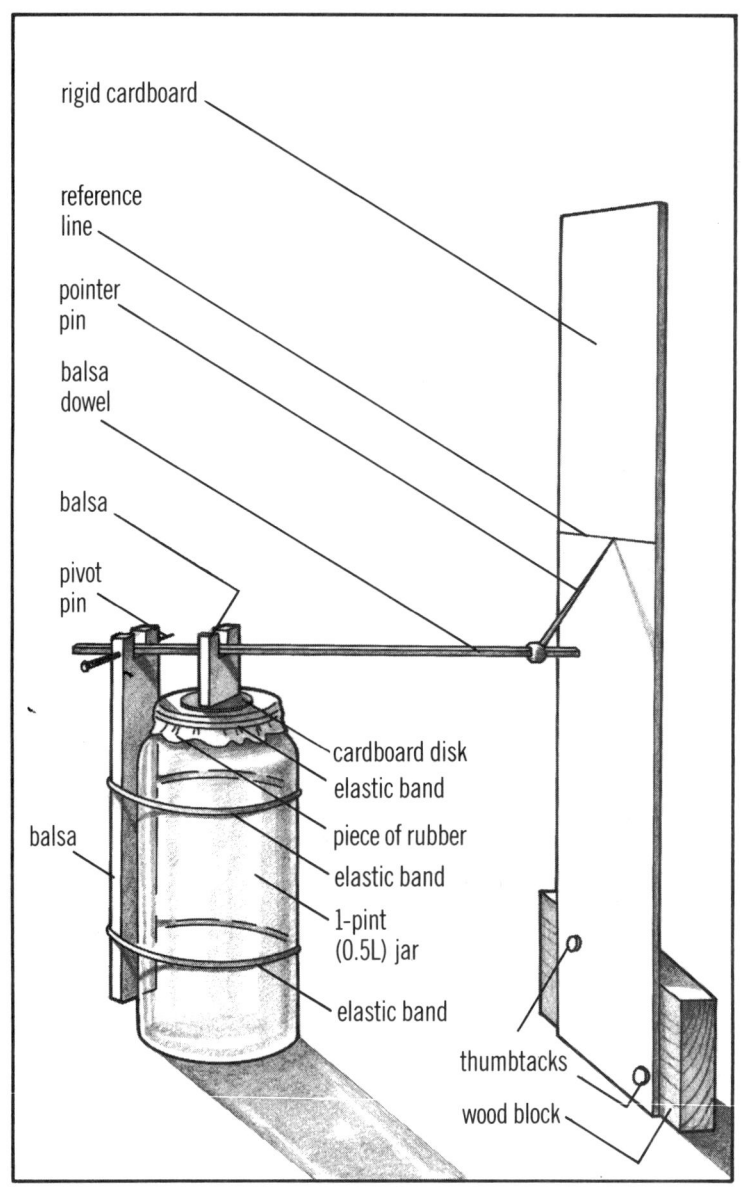

Figure 2. A demonstration aneroid barometer

wide, and long enough so that when it is attached to the jar it is 1 inch (2.5 cm) taller than the jar; cut a wedge out of the top

2 pins

a thin balsa dowel or stick, about 12 inches (30 cm) long

a thin cardboard disk, 1 inch (2.5 cm) in diameter

2 thumbtacks

a block of wood, about 4 inches (10 cm) long, 2 inches (5 cm) wide, and 2 inches (5 cm) high

a strip of rigid cardboard, 2 inches (5 cm) wide, and long enough so that when it is mounted on the block of wood it is about 4 inches (10 cm) taller than the jar

To assemble the barometer:

1. Run a bead of glue around the outside rim of the jar. Stretch the piece of rubber over the mouth of the jar and press down on the center to force a little air out of the jar. Fasten the rubber tightly with an elastic band and seal it by pressing the edge against the glue. There should be a slight depression in the center of the rubber cover. (You have created a partial vacuum.) Let the glue dry.

2. Glue the 1/2 x 1 inch (1 x 2.5 cm) piece of balsa onto the cardboard disk so that the wedge is on top. Let the glue dry.

3. Glue the assembled cardboard disk onto the center of the rubber cover. Let the glue dry.

4. Place the long piece of balsa against the jar. The wedge on top of the balsa should be lined up with the wedge on the small piece of balsa in the center of the rubber cover. When the notches are aligned, use two rubber bands to fasten the balsa to the jar.

5. Stick one pin through one end of the balsa dowel so that it points horizontally. Rest the other end of the dowel in the two notches. Push the second pin through the long piece of balsa and the dowel to act as a pivot so that the dowel can move easily.

6. Use the two thumbtacks to fasten the strip of cardboard to the center of the side of the block of wood.

7. Place the assembled instrument where it will not be disturbed. Line up the cardboard so that the pointer pin does not quite touch it. Draw a line on the cardboard at the level of the pin.

The barometer is now ready for use. The line you drew is your reference. When there is a change in atmospheric pressure, the pin will move above or below the line. If the pressure is higher, the air will push harder on the rubber cover and the pin will drop below the reference line. You may even be able to see a greater depression in the rubber cover. When the atmospheric pressure decreases, the push on the rubber will be less and the pin will rise.

The atmosphere is in constant motion: cold air, warm air, moist air, dry air moving in and out of areas all the time. Cold, dry air is heavier and exerts more pressure than warm, moist air. Therefore, during a period of high pressure the weather is likely to be fair, but during a period of low pressure the weather is likely to be stormy. You can use your barometer to roughly estimate the barometric pressure, but for a long-term home weather station, a commercial aneroid barometer is recommended. Inexpensive, satisfactory barometers can be bought in hardware and housewares stores or from one of the companies listed at the end of the book.

The barometer you buy should be adjusted for the altitude of your home weather station according to the instructions provided by the manufacturer. If you live at sea level, the normal atmospheric pressure is 29.9 inches (76.2 cm). But as you go higher and higher, less air above you is pressing down so the atmospheric pressure is less. An easy way to adjust the barometer is to listen to the local weather broadcast on a clear, dry day and set your instrument to the barometric pressure announced. To keep track of the changes in barometric pressure, you should read and record the pressure at the same times at least twice a day. Gently tap the glass cover of the barometer before recording your readings.

SUGGESTED ACTIVITIES

1. Devise a way to use your air pressure–experiment equipment to blow up a balloon. Replace the cork with a balloon.

2. Devise a way to use a plastic bag, a straw, and a twistem to lift a book.

3. Use a commercial barometer to calibrate your homemade barometer.

4. Find out how sensitive (accurate) your homemade barometer is by comparing the air pressure it registers with the air pressure registered on a commercial barometer over several days or weeks. Graph your comparisons.

5. Gently tap the glass cover of a commercial barometer to see how the indicator moves. Record whether the barometer is rising or falling. Use your observations to predict if there will be a change in the weather. Graph your observations and predictions. What conclusions can you draw?

6. Take your barometer to the top of a many-storied building or high hill. Record the difference in barometric pressure from ground level to the top.

Record the barometric pressure at various heights of the building or hill. Graph your observations to determine the change in barometric pressure for every 10 feet (3 m) of elevation.

7. Demonstrate how a barometer can be used as an altimeter to determine the height (altitude) of a many-storied building or a hill. (Barometric pressure falls about 0.01 inch [0.25 mm] for every 10 feet [3 m] above sea level.)

8. Find out if you can use a piece of aluminum foil or some other flexible material instead of the rubber in the homemade barometer.

9. Make a bottle barometer. Use a narrow-necked bottle (ketchup bottle) and a shallow bowl with a flat bottom. Put a little water with a few drops of food coloring into the bowl. Fill the bottle to the brim with colored water. Place your thumb or the palm of your hand over the mouth of the bottle and invert the bottle in the bowl of water. Some of the water will run out into the bowl. Why?

Draw lines every ⅛ of an inch (0.3 cm) on a 4-inch-long (10 cm) narrow strip of paper. Tape the paper to the side of the bottle so that the middle of the strip is at the level of the water. Observe the changes in barometric pressure as indicated by the rising and falling level of the water. Compare the responses of this barometer with those of your other barometers.

HOT AIR, COLD AIR

The air around us is constantly changing. Sometimes it's heavier, sometimes it's lighter; sometimes it's wetter, sometimes it's drier; sometimes it's hotter, sometimes it's colder. Air is heated by the sun's rays that pass through it. When there is more sunshine, the *temperature* (degree of hotness or coldness) of the air is usually greater; when there is less sunshine, the temperature of the air is often lower. The amount of sunlight that reaches the atmosphere varies with the seasons (see Figure

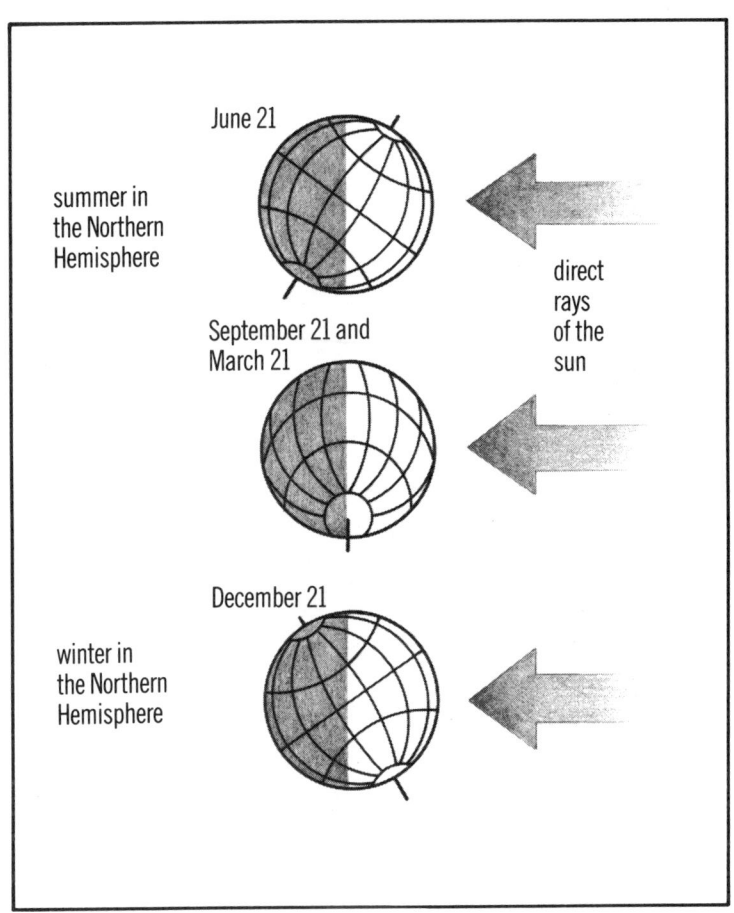

Figure 3. Seasonal changes in the direct rays of the sun

3). During the summer, the atmosphere receives more direct sunlight and for more hours each day than in the winter (see Figure 4). Therefore, the temperature of the air normally is higher in summer than in winter.

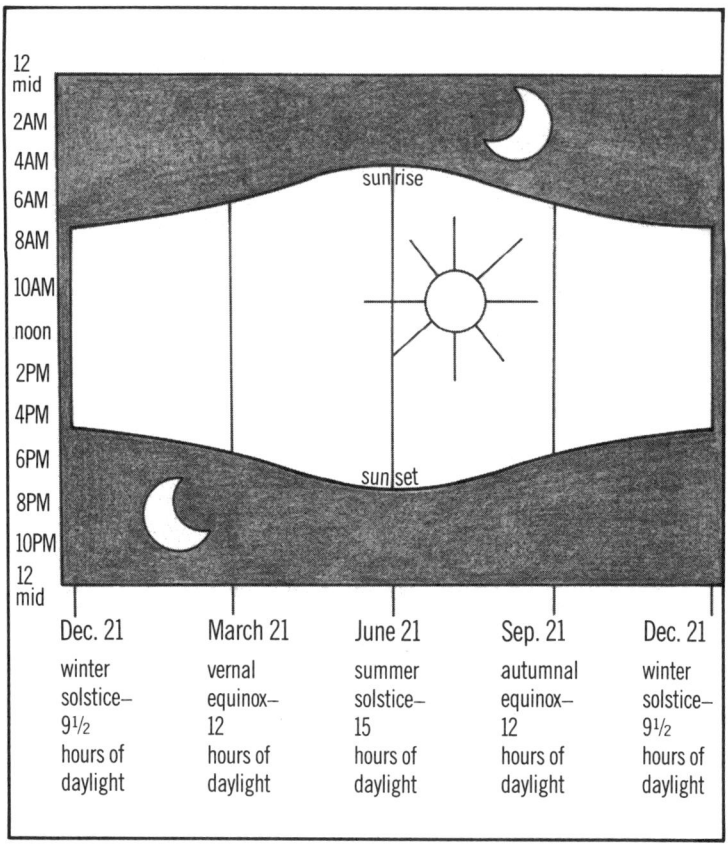

Figure 4. The amount of sunlight in Washington, D.C., throughout the year

On cloudy days, when the lower atmosphere gets less sunshine than on clear days, the temperature of the air at the earth's surface is often lower. And sometimes things other than clouds can block the sunshine and lower the temperature.

This was the case in 1816, "the year without a summer." On April 5, 1815, the Tambora volcano, on the island of Sumbawa, Indonesia, exploded, killing an estimated twelve thousand people. Volcanic ash and dust were spewed high into the atmosphere, blocking out much of the sun's rays. The winds carried the debris around the world for more than a year. As a result, there were many very cloudy days, keeping the sunlight from heating the air normally. The temperature of the air was unusally low all summer, and on the east coast (the only place in the United States where records were kept at that time) the following events occurred:

June 7, 1816	— A snowstorm in Danville, Vermont, caused drifts 20 inches (50 cm) deep, and it snowed as far south as Boston.
July 8–9, 1816	— There was frost in low places throughout New England.
August 22, 1816	— There was a damaging frost in low places from New England to North Carolina.
September 27, 1816	— A black frost over most of New England killed the still unripened corn.

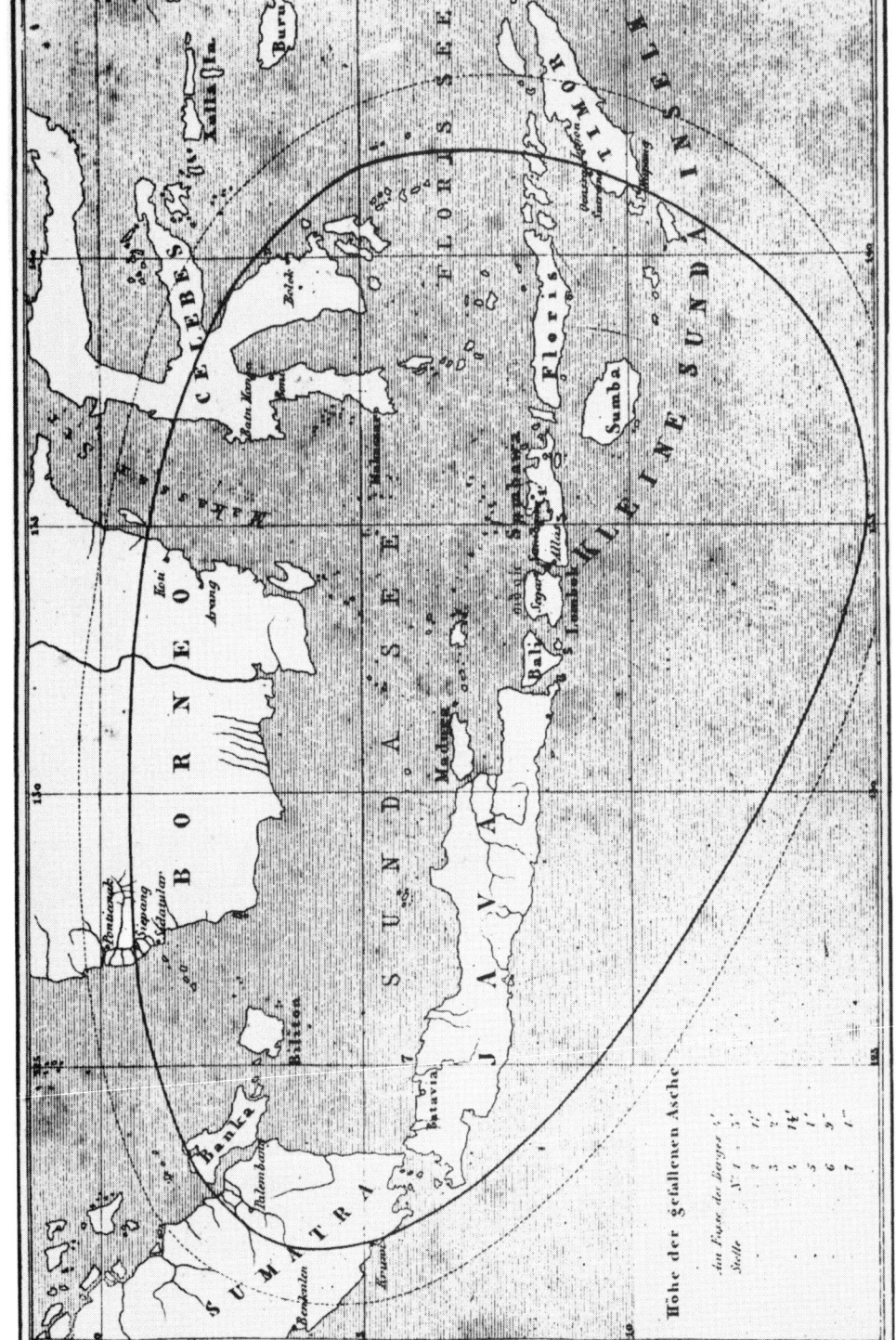

Facing page: the Tambora volcano on an island in Indonesia erupted in 1815 and caused unusual weather conditions all over the world. The map shows the area of ashfall from the volcano.
Above: one of the strange weather occurrences resulting from the eruption was a major snowstorm in New England in June, 1816.

The heat *energy* of the sun's rays that reach the earth is generated by the sun. The temperature on the surface of the sun is estimated at about 11,000°F (6,000°C). But it takes radiation from the sun about eight and a third minutes to reach the earth. During that long trip, most of the heat is lost in space.

Temperatures on the earth's surface vary about 214°F (146°C). New records of temperature extremes continue to be set. The coldest place on earth is Antarctica, and the hottest place is the Libyan desert in Africa. In the United States, the present record temperatures are:

−80°F (−62°C) — Prospect Creek, Alaska
January 23, 1971
134°F (57°C) — Death Valley, California
July 10, 1913

TRANSFERENCE OF HEAT • You can find out how heat is transferred. Use two glasses or bowls of different sizes; one should be small enough to fit inside the other. Partly fill the smaller container with very hot water from the tap. Test the temperature of the water with your finger. Partly fill the larger one with very cold water. Test the temperature of the water with your finger. Place the smaller container into the larger one. Let both containers stand a half-hour. Test the temperature of the water in each container again. What happened?

Scientists have found that heat is transferred from a warmer body to a cooler body until both are at the same temperature. You can find out what hap-

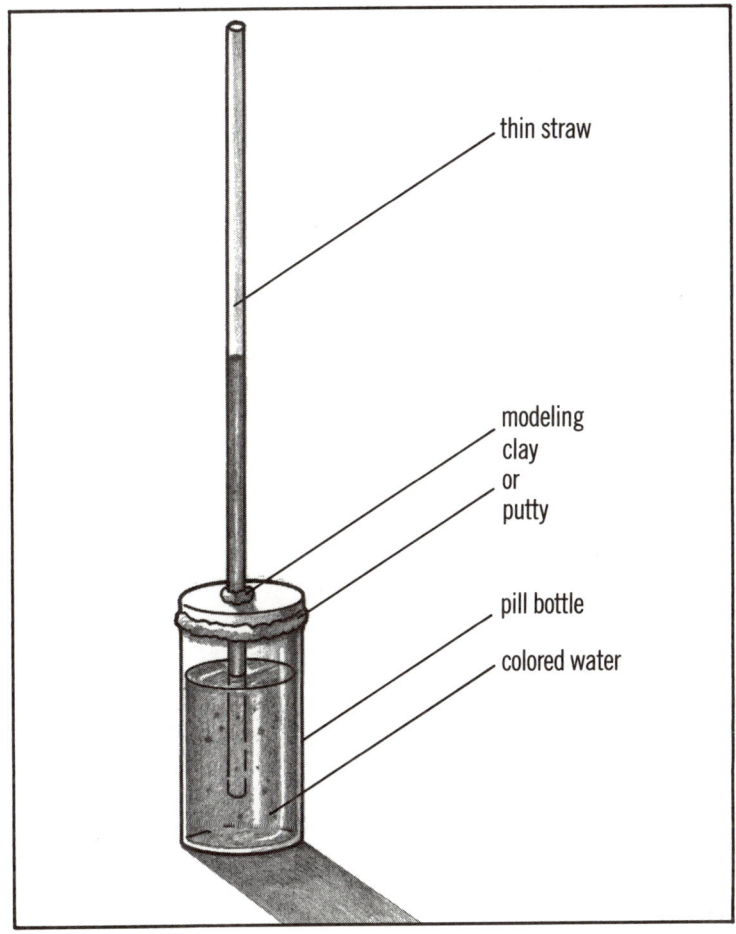

Figure 5. A demonstration thermometer

pens to a liquid that is heated and cooled. Refer to Figure 5. You will need:

a paring knife or other sharp pointed tool
a small pill bottle with a plastic cap

a thin, clear straw (a cocktail straw)
modeling clay or putty
water with a drop of food coloring in it
a container of very hot water
a crayon or felt-tip pen
a container of very cold water

Punch a small hole in the plastic cap and push the straw partway through it. Seal any opening around the straw with modeling clay or putty. Fill the pill bottle with colored water. Place the cap on the bottle with part of the straw in the colored water. Use modeling clay or putty to seal the cap tightly.

Place the pill bottle into the container of very hot water. Let it stand a few minutes. What happens? Mark the level of the liquid in the straw with a crayon or felt-tip pen.

Place the pill bottle into the container of very cold water. Let it stand a few minutes. What happens? Mark the new level of the liquid in the straw.

THERMOMETERS • You have just made a *thermometer*, an instrument to measure temperature. A thermometer works on the principle that a liquid expands when heated and contracts when cooled. When you put the thermometer into the container of hot water, the liquid in the pill bottle was heated and it expanded, rising in the straw. When you put the thermometer into the container of cold water, the liquid in the pill bottle cooled and it contracted, dropping in the straw. To be able to tell how hot or how cold the liquid in the pill bottle is, you would need a scale marked in degrees.

The first commonly used scale was devised by Gabriel Fahrenheit, a German scientist. Fahrenheit believed that the coldest temperature possible is the point at which seawater freezes. This he labeled 0°. Then he used the temperature of the human body for the top of his scale. This he labeled 100°. (We now know that normal body temperature is 98.6°F.) Then he divided his scale into 100 equal steps, or degrees. On the Fahrenheit scale, at normal atmospheric pressure, fresh water boils at 212° and freezes at 32°. If the temperature of the air is very cold, we say it is below zero or minus so many degrees. At first, Fahrenheit used colored alcohol for his thermometer, but in 1714 he changed to mercury.

Some people considered Fahrenheit's scale clumsy because there are 180 degrees between the freezing point and boiling point of water. In 1742, the Swedish scientist Anders Celsius devised a simpler scale. In the Celsius scale, water freezes at 0° and boils at 100°. There are only 100 degrees between the two points instead of 180. A Fahrenheit degree is smaller than a Celsius degree; it takes more Fahrenheit degrees to measure the same change in temperature. Usually we do not write out "degrees Fahrenheit" and "degrees Celsius" each time we record temperature; we just use the degree symbols and the first letters, °F and °C.

As with barometers, there are also thermometers without liquids. Aneroid thermometers work because of the expansion and contraction of thin strips of metal when heated or cooled. A pointer is attached to the metal and a scale is placed behind the pointer. There are also thermometers which can be set to register the lowest (minimum) temperature and the highest (maximum) temperature for a given period of time. These are useful for reporting weather data because you don't have to stay up all night to find out how low the temperature drops. The coldest temperature since the last reading is recorded, and the observer can read it whenever convenient and then reset the thermometer.

For your home weather station, you may wish to obtain a good inexpensive thermometer. If you are interested in temperature extremes, buy a maximum-minimum thermometer. These are available where you get your barometer. To get the best possible reading of the temperature of the air, place your thermometer out of direct sunlight and not too close to your house. (Heat from a building is transferred to the air around it.) Read and record the temperature at the same times at least twice a day.

SUGGESTED ACTIVITIES

1. Use a commercial thermometer to calibrate your pill-bottle thermometer. First determine a high temperature, then a low temperature. Predict where the marks for the intervening degrees should be drawn. Use the commercial thermometer to check your results.

2. Make two other thermometers. Use a long thin jar (olive jar) and a thin straw (cocktail straw) for one. Use a pill bottle and a thick straw (regular drinking straw) for the other. Calibrate each thermometer. Determine the differences, if any, in the scales.

3. Use other liquids such as colored rubbing alcohol in a pill-bottle thermometer. Calibrate each thermometer. Determine the differences, if any, in the scales.

4. Keep a record of the number of daylight hours (from sunrise to sunset) throughout the year for your hometown. Correlate the average daily temperature you record each week or each month with the average number of daylight hours for that period of time. Graph your results.

5. Find and record the temperature of the air in various places in the vicinity of your home, for example: under a tree; on an upstairs windowsill; in a hole a few inches into the ground; near water such as a stream, a fountain, or a swimming pool; in a carport; over a sunny sidewalk.

6. On a weekend or during vacation, record the temperature every hour from the time you get up in the morning until you go to bed at night. Graph your observations. Repeat this experience several times. What conclusions can you draw? For example:

- What is the hottest time of the day?
- What is the coldest time of the day?
- Does the air cool off more quickly or more slowly than it warms up?
- Does the graph look the same at different seasons of the year?
- Does the temperature of the air change more rapidly on a sunny day or a cloudy day?

MOISTURE IN THE AIR

Sometimes the air is wetter; sometimes the air is drier. How does moisture get into the air, and why does it fall back to earth? You can find out how this happens by boiling some water. Use a kettle—a glass kettle will break if boiled dry. Partly fill the kettle with water and heat it on a stove. Watch carefully, especially at the mouth of the spout, but don't get too close. What do you see? Turn off the heat.

You know that when a liquid is heated, it expands. A liquid heated enough expands so much that it becomes a gas. This happens with water when it boils. If you kept heating the kettle, all the water in it would boil away and escape into the air as water vapor, which is a gas.

Turn the heat back on under the kettle. Wait till the water boils. Use tongs to hold an aluminum foil pan about 2 inches (5 cm) from the spout. What do you see on the pan? Turn the heat off.

The aluminum foil pan was cooler than the water vapor escaping from the kettle. The hot water vapor was cooled by contact with the pan and turned back into liquid, and drops of water ran down the pan. It rained!

In nature, this process takes place continually on a worldwide scale. Water from the oceans, seas, lakes, rivers, and ponds evaporates and escapes into the air. The warmer the air, the more vapor it can hold. Warm, moist air rises and is blown far and wide. When this air cools by coming in contact with cold air, under certain conditions, the water vapor in the warm air condenses, first forming clouds and then falling back to earth as rain—or snow, or sleet, or hail. The rain, or melted snow, sleet, or hail runs into streams which join to make rivers that flow into the oceans, where it can evaporate again. (Actually some of the water evaporates in the streams and rivers.) All living things, all plants and animals, also give off water vapor. Each time you breathe out, some moisture escapes into the air. To see this moisture, hold a mirror close to your mouth and breathe out. The water cycle is endless: a molecule of water

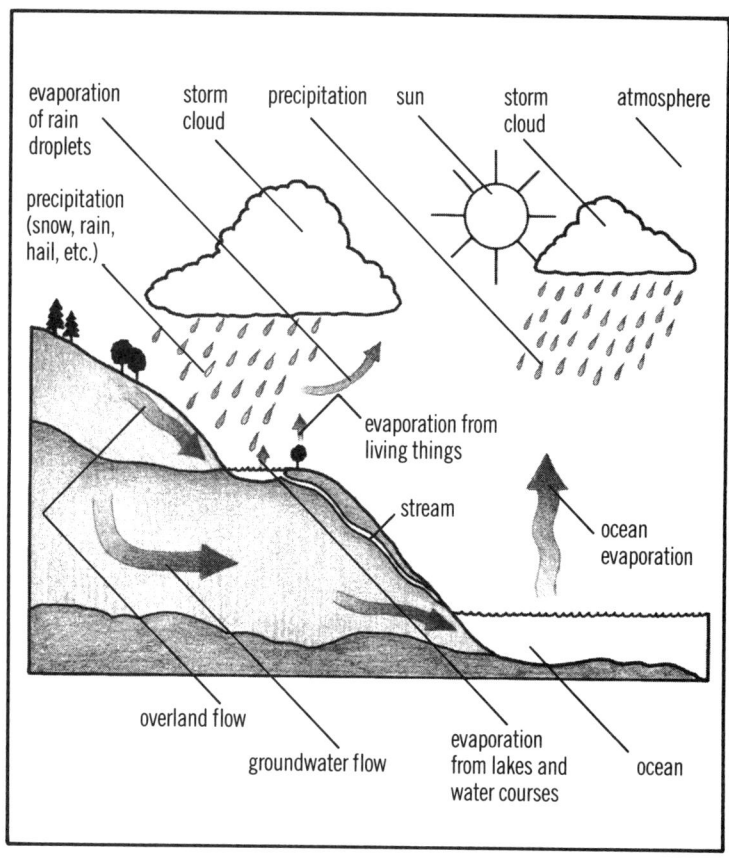

Figure 6. The water cycle

is evaporated and condenses over and over again. Figure 6 illustrates the water cycle.

RELATIVE HUMIDITY • The amount of moisture in the air at any given time compared to the greatest amount possible at the same temperature is called the *relative humidity*. ("Humidity" comes from a Latin word meaning "to be moist.") Warm air can hold more moisture than cold air. When air at a certain temperature holds as much moisture as possible, we say the relative humidity is 100%. The air has reached its *saturation point*. If the air holds only half the moisture it could hold at that temperature, the relative humidity is 50%. If it contains only a quarter, the relative humidity is 25%. At 32°F (0°C), 1.3 cubic yards (1 cu m) of air can hold 0.16 ounce (4.9 g) of water. At 86°F, (30°C) the same amount of air can hold 1 ounce (30 g) of water.

Temperature	Amount of Water per 1.3 Cubic Yards (1 cu m)	Relative Humidity
32°F (0°C)	0.16 ounce (4.9 g)	100%
32°F (0°C)	0.08 ounce (2.4 g)	50%
32°F (0°C)	0.04 ounce (1.2 g)	25%
—	—	—
86°F (30°C)	1 ounce (30 g)	100%
86°F (30°C)	0.50 ounce (15 g)	50%
86°F (30°C)	0.25 ounce (7.6 g)	25%

The greater the relative humidity—the more moisture in the air—the less comfortable people are. You may have heard the expression, "It's not the heat, it's the humidity!" When we are hot, we perspire: we give off moisture (sweat) that cools the skin as it evaporates. But when the relative humidity is high, the sweat cannot evaporate as readily and the body cannot cool off comfortably.

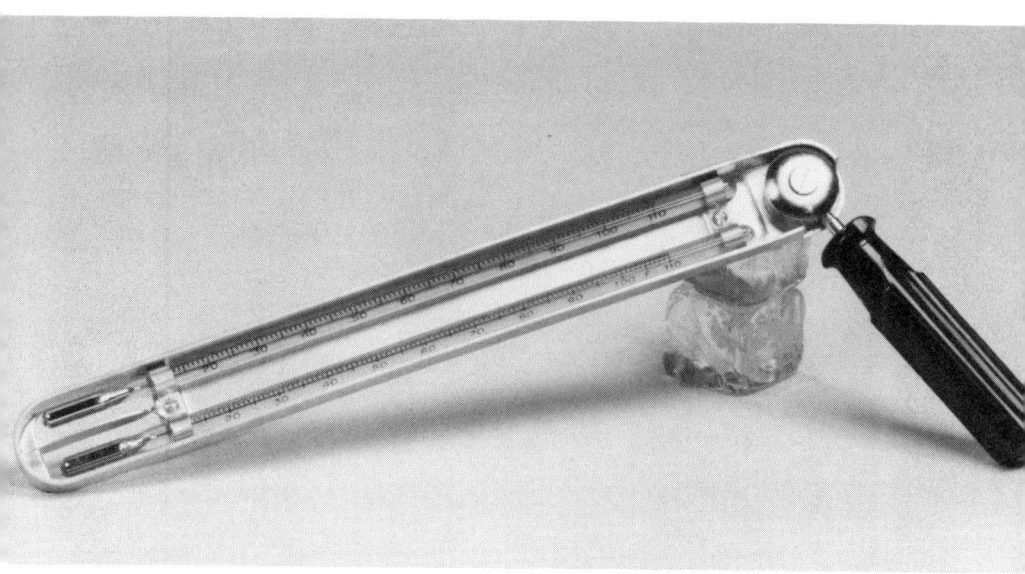

A sling psychrometer measures relative humidity.

Relative humidity can be measured by an instrument called a *hygrometer*. The simplest hygrometer—*sling psychrometer*—consists of two thermometers mounted together with a handle attached on a chain. One thermometer is ordinary. The other has a cloth wick over its bulb and is called a wet-bulb thermometer.

When a reading is to be taken, the wick is first dipped in water and then the instrument is whirled around. During the whirling, the water evaporates from the wick, cooling the wet-bulb thermometer. Then the temperatures of both thermometers are read.

If the surrounding air is dry, more moisture evaporates from the wick, cooling the wet-bulb thermometer more so there is a greater difference between the temperatures of the two thermometers. If the surrounding air is very moist, there is little evaporation and the difference between the two temperatures is less. If the surrounding air is holding as much moisture as possible—if the relative humidity is 100%—there is no difference between the two temperatures. Meteorologists have worked out charts of these differences for each degree of temperature so that the observer can find the relative humidity easily. A sample is shown below.

PARTIAL RELATIVE HUMIDITY CHART
FOR 86°F (30°C)

Difference Between Dry Bulb and Wet Bulb Temperatures	*Relative Humidity*
None	100%
0.9°F (0.5°C)	96%
1.8°F (1.0°C)	93%
2.7°F (1.5°C)	89%
—	—
16.2°F (9.0°C)	44%
17.1°F (9.5°C)	42%
—	—
26.1°F (14.5°C)	19%
27.0°F (15.0°C)	17%
—	—
32.4°F (18.0°C)	5%

You can make a sling psychrometer by using two commercial thermometers. Wrap the bulb of one tightly with a piece of cloth. Attach the thermometers to a narrow, thin board with wire or strong tape. Drill a hole in the top of the board and attach a wooden handle to the board with a short piece of chain.

Your homemade psychrometer may be clumsy to use, and it may be just as economical to buy a commercial one if you want to include the relative humidity in your daily home-weather-station reports. If your local stores do not have a sling psychrometer, you can order one from one of the weather instrument suppliers listed on page 104. A detailed relative humidity chart usually is included when you purchase a psychrometer.

PRECIPITATION • As warm, moist air rises, it slowly cools. When it cools so much that its relative humidity reaches 100%, clouds form and, under certain conditions, rain or snow comes down. Just how much moisture falls to earth depends on such factors as how much moisture is contained in the clouds and how fast the clouds pass overhead (how fast the wind blows them away). Rainfall is measured in inches or millimeters. The National Weather Service measures rainfall in inches. One inch of rain is the amount of rain that would form a layer 1 inch deep on level ground if none of the water ran off or seeped into the ground.

Record rainfalls can be reported for a single storm, or a twenty-four-hour period, or a month, or a year. The record rainfalls for the world and the United States respectively are:

Greatest in twenty-four hours
73.62 inches—Reunion Island, Indian Ocean; March 15–16, 1952
43.00 inches—Alvin, Texas; July 25–26, 1979

Greatest in one month
366.14 inches—Assam, India; July 1861
107.00 inches—Kauai, Hawaii; March 1942

Greatest in one year
905.12 inches—Assam, India; 1861
578.00 inches—Kauai, Hawaii; 1950

Since extremes do not give a true picture of the local climate, we depend on average rainfall records to describe a place or plan activities. The wettest place on earth is Mt. Waialeale on Kauai, Hawaii, where for forty-six years the average annual rainfall was 460 inches. The driest place on earth is Arica, Chile, where for forty-three years the average rainfall was 0.02 inch and for 171 months, from October 1903 to December 1917, no rain fell at all.

Snowfall records are also kept, and for the United States the current records are:

Greatest in twenty-four hours
75.8 inches—Silver Lake, Colorado; April 14–15, 1921

Greatest in a single storm
  189 inches—Mt. Shasta, California;
    February 13–19, 1959
Greatest in a month
  390 inches—Tamarack, California;
    January 1911
Greatest in a season
  1,122 inches—Mt. Rainier, Washington;
    1971–1972

BUILDING A RAIN GAUGE • You can make a rain gauge for your weather station. Use a tall, narrow clear bottle (an olive jar, for example). Use a fine-pointed crayon or waterproof pen to draw lines every inch from the bottom of the jar up the side. Divide each inch into ten equal parts. Place the rain gauge in a sturdy container out in the open where it will not get any runoff from buildings or trees and where it will not be tipped over.

Your rain gauge will not be accurate, especially for small amounts of rainfall, for several reasons. First, the lines you draw may not be precise. Second, if you don't read the gauge as soon as it stops raining, some water may evaporate. Empty the gauge after each reading and dry the inside. Your gauge will give you a fair record of the rainfall, but if you want a better instrument, you can buy an inexpensive plastic rain gauge from a local store or from a supply house. You can include a record of the rainfall in your home-weather-station procedures.

SUGGESTED ACTIVITIES

1. Find out and graph the rate of evaporation under various conditions:

- on a sunny day
- on a cloudy day
- on a calm day
- on a windy day
- from a container with a narrow mouth
- from a container with a wide mouth
- in the basement or ground floor
- in the attic or top floor

2. Explain why people sometimes feel more comfortable in Phoenix, Arizona, when the temperature is 104°F (40°C) than in New York City when the temperature is 77°F (25°C).

3. Compare the rainfall registered by your homemade rain gauge with the amount recorded by a commerical rain gauge.

4. Use containers of various sizes as rain gauges. Graph the amount of rainfall recorded by each gauge. Account for the differences, if any.

5. Use your sling psychrometer to find the relative humidity on the same day at various locations, such as:

- outside your house
- inside your house
- in the school yard

- near an indoor swimming pool
- in a park
- near a lake or river or at the seashore

Graph the results and evaluate your data to determine what factors in the environment affect the local relative humidity.

6. Make a decorative simple hygrometer. Use a piece of white blotting paper or a thick, white paper towel. Cut out a design such as the silhouette of a person with an umbrella. Make a solution of two parts cobalt chloride and one part table salt. Dip the paper into the solution; the paper will turn pink and remain pink as long as it is wet. When the paper dries, it will turn blue. Hang the figure on a hook or by a string so that air can circulate around it. Your simple hygrometer will indicate whether the air in the room is moist or dry.

7. Make another type of hygrometer using a long human hair. The hair expands when it is moist and contracts when it is dry. Wash the hair thoroughly in alcohol and blot it dry. Make a stand with an upright, a vertical piece of wood, longer than the hair. Attach a cardboard or paper scale to the upright. Use instant glue to fasten a needle to a bolt. Use instant glue to attach the bolt to one end of the hair. Attach the other end of the hair to the top of the upright so that it can move freely and the needle can point to the scale.

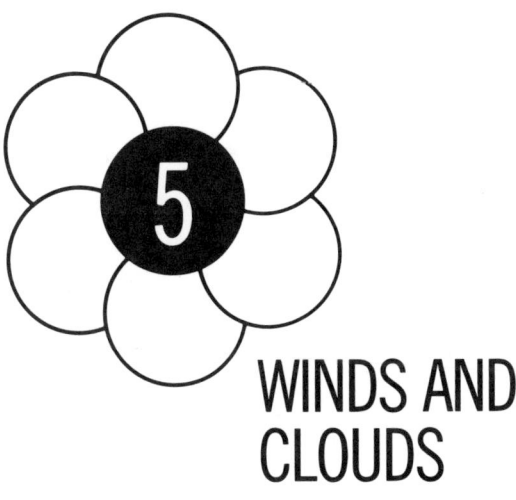

WINDS AND CLOUDS

For many years, the Canadian government has been trying to get the government of the United States to stop acid rain from falling on the provinces of Ontario and Quebec. *Acid rain* is rain that contains sulfuric acid; it destroys freshwater life and land plants, especially trees. Why should the United States be concerned? Isn't it Canada's problem?

Not entirely! Most of the sulfuric acid comes from factories in the northern part of the United States. These factories burn coal that con-

Facing page: Acid rain—rain containing sulfuric acid—is a serious problem. Factories that pollute the air are a major cause of acid rain. *Above:* a research station designed to measure acid rain caused by air pollution

tains large amounts of sulfur. Burning coal gives off sulfur dioxide gas, which rises up the smokestacks and escapes into the air. Sulfur dioxide combines with the moisture in the air to form sulfuric acid. The winds blow the polluted moisture over the northern states and the Canadian provinces, where it falls back to earth as acid rain.

Wind is air in motion, and the winds follow certain patterns. When air near the equator is heated by the intense rays of the sun passing through it and by contact with warm ground and oceans, the air expands, becomes lighter, and rises. Cooler air flows in to take the place of the warm air. This cooler air, in its turn, is warmed, expands, and rises.

You can see how this happens. You will need:

a balloon
a narrow-necked bottle (a ketchup bottle, for example)
a container of very hot water
a container of very cold water

Fasten the balloon over the neck of the bottle. Place the bottle into the hot water. Watch what happens to the balloon. Now place the bottle into the cold water. What happens to the balloon? Put the bottle back into the hot water. What happens?

When the air in the bottle is heated by contact with the hot water, the air expands and rises. The hot air rises up into the balloon and inflates it. When the air is cooled by contact with the cold water, the air contracts and sinks. The air sinks back into the bottle and the balloon deflates. When the air is reheated, the air rises again. This is similar to what happens to the air surrounding the earth. The air is heated at the equator and rises and drifts toward the polar regions. The cooler air from the polar regions sinks and flows toward the equator to take the place of the rising hot air.

WIND PATTERNS • If the earth did not rotate, the surface winds in the northern hemisphere (the cooler air) would blow from north to south. But the earth is spinning very fast—about 1,000 miles (1,600 km) per hour at the equator and about 700 miles (1,120 km) per hour in the latitude of Philadelphia, PA, Springfield, IL., and Denver, CO. This rotation of the earth causes the air to follow the wind patterns shown by the arrows in Figure 7.

Many local factors may cause changes in these large general patterns. If there is an unevenness in the heating of the air, the warm air rising and the cooler air flowing in can create a local wind. For example, winds can be caused because land warms faster than water during the day. Therefore, the warmer air over the land rises and the cooler air from over the ocean flows in to take its place, causing a "sea breeze." At night, the land cools faster than the water. Then the warmer air over the ocean rises and the cooler air from over the land flows in resulting in a "land breeze."

Similar situations occur in the mountains, where the tops of the mountains heat up faster than the valleys in the daytime and cool off faster at night.

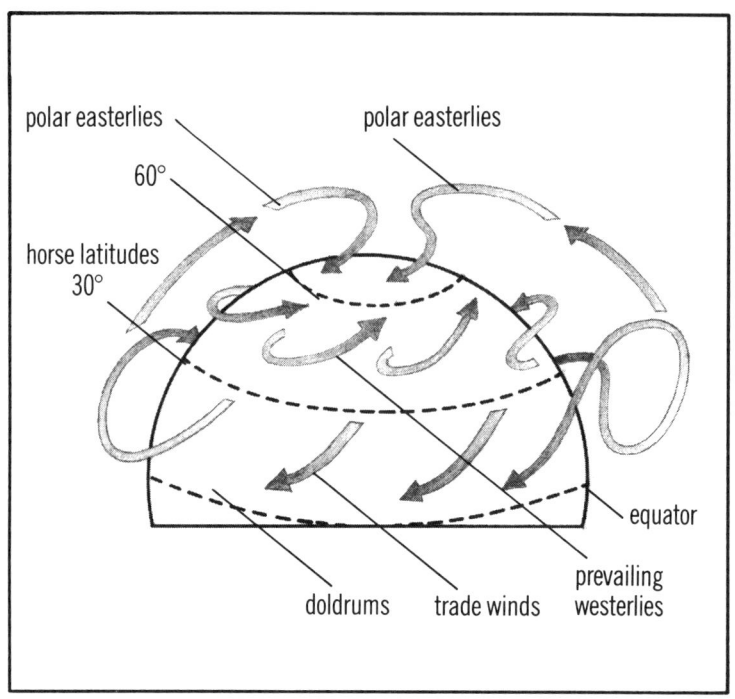

Figure 7. Wind patterns in the Northern Hemisphere

Local winds and breezes can be caused even by small hills and dales, by small ponds or lakes, or by alternate plowed fields of dark earth, which heat up faster than the grassy fields next to them.

BUILDING A WIND VANE • It is easy to tell the direction from which the wind is blowing. If there is a flag flying, the wind will make it billow in the same direction as the wind is blowing. A simple wind-direction instrument is called a *wind vane*. It is an arrow attached to a support so that the arrow can move freely in the breeze. The support also contains letters to indicate the wind directions: E (east), N (north), W (west), and S (south). Wind vanes (also called weather vanes) are common sights, especially in rural areas where they are often used for decorating barns and steeples. Some are imaginative, with an animal, such as a rooster, or a man's face replacing the ordinary arrow.

You can make a wind vane for your weather station. Refer to Figure 8. You will need:

*a 10-inch (25-cm) piece of straight wire
(from a wire hanger)
a piece of heavy paper or thin cardboard
(like a file folder)
a crayon or marking pen
scissors
tape
2 plastic straws
the cap from a ballpoint pen*

On the paper or cardboard, draw the head and tail of the arrow. Each should be about 4 inches (10 cm) long and about 2-1/4 inches (5.6 cm) wide. Cut them out and use tape to attach them to either end of a straw.

Tape the center of the straw to the tip of the pen cap.

Cut the other straw into four equal lengths. Mark one "E," another "N," the third "W," and the fourth "S." Tape them to the piece of wire about 4 inches

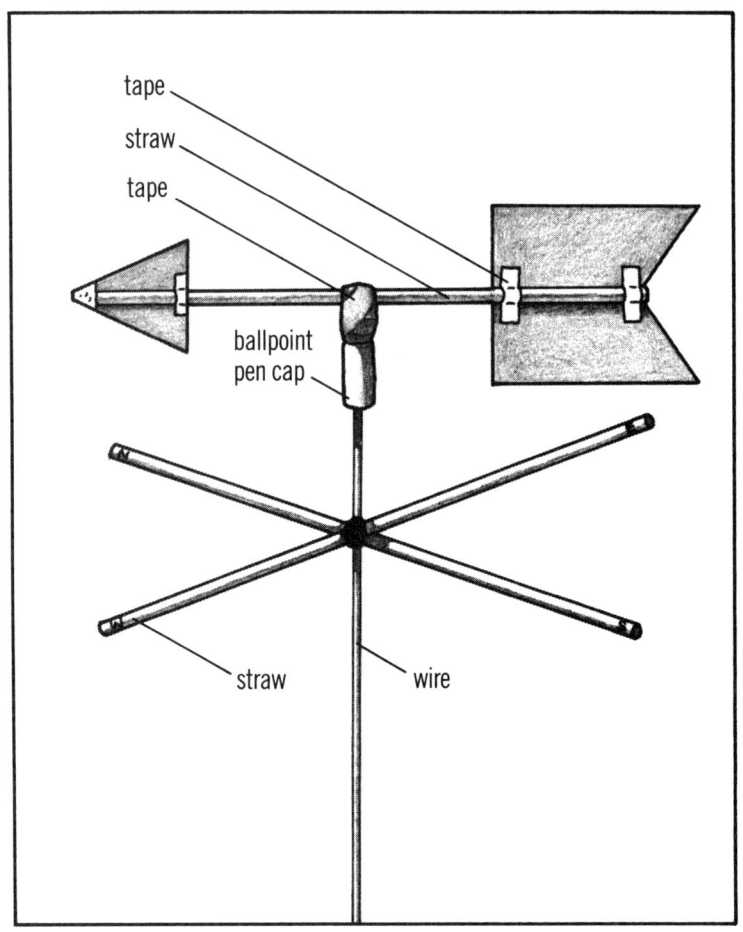

Figure 8. A demonstration wind vane

(10 cm) from the top. They should be at right angles to each other.

Put the wire into the pen cap.

You can hold the wind vane in your hand, or you can mount it on a suitable object out in the open.

Wind vanes measure wind direction. Many vanes have interesting and unusual objects on top and are used to decorate barns and roofs.

Use a compass to be sure that the directions are correct: N should face north. Winds are always labeled in the direction from which they blow. Thus, when the head of your arrow is pointing south and the tail is facing north, there is a north wind blowing. You can include wind direction in your twice-daily weather report.

The direction and speed of winds were, and still are, very important to sailing ships. Before there were steamboats, motorboats, or nuclear-powered boats, sailors, unless they used manpower to propel the boats by means of oars, depended on winds blowing on sails to move a boat across the water. Navigators knew the wind-belt patterns. So, if they wanted to cross from Europe to America, they took advantage of the northeast trade winds to speed them across the Atlantic. That is why Columbus first landed on a Caribbean island in the heart of the trade winds belt.

THE JET STREAM • Just as sailors learned about wind belts on the surface of the earth, aviators, flying over the Pacific Ocean during World War II, discovered a wind belt between 20,000 feet (6,000 m) and 40,000 feet (12,000 m) up. This is the *jet stream*, a tubelike belt of winds moving at very high speeds. Some scientists believe the jet stream is caused by the coming together of large masses of warm and cool air. The jet stream wanders north and south throughout the year. In the Northern Hemisphere in the winter, the jet stream can travel across the southern United States as far south as southern Texas and Florida. In the summer, it moves farther north and can be found over the states along the Canadian border. The jet stream is snakelike: it twists its way across the continent, sometimes very high, sometimes lower, sometimes farther north, sometimes farther south, but nearly always from west to east.

THE BEAUFORT SCALE • Even though people could easily determine the direction of the winds, they did not agree on how to measure the speed of the winds until 1805. In that year the British admiral Francis Beaufort used his observations of the effect of wind speed on the sails of a ship to create a wind-speed scale. Because sailors measured speed at sea in knots, the Beaufort wind scale was set up in knots. A knot is 1.15 miles (1.84 km) per hour. People usually talk about a 30-mile-per-hour or 50-mile-per-hour wind, but the National Weather Service records winds in knots.

If a flag is flying, you can estimate the wind speed from the appearance of the flag (see Figure 9).

BUILDING AN ANEMOMETER • We do not have to rely on mere observation to measure wind speed; we can use an instrument called an *anemometer* (*anemo* is the Greek word for "wind"). The simplest anemometer works like a pinwheel. The wind pushing against its cups spins the instrument, and the number of turns it makes in a second or minute is recorded and translated into knots or into miles per hour. During a hurricane, wind gusts can reach 180 miles (290 km) per hour, or 160 knots, or more. The strongest surface

THE BEAUFORT SCALE

Beaufort Number	Knots	Miles per Hour	Km per Hour	Description	Observation on Land
0	0–1	0–1	0–1	Calm	Smoke rises straight up
1	1–3	1–3	1–5	Light air	Smoke drifts; tree leaves barely move
2	4–6	4–7	6–11	Slight breeze	Leaves rustle; wind felt on face
3	7–10	8–12	12–19	Gentle breeze	Leaves and twigs in motion; bits of paper and dust rise from the ground
4	11–16	13–18	20–28	Moderate breeze	Small branches move
5	17–21	19–24	29–38	Fresh breeze	Small trees sway; dust clouds rise
6	22–27	25–31	39–49	Strong breeze	Large branches sway; difficult to use umbrellas
7	28–33	32–38	50–61	Moderate gale	Whole trees in motion; difficult to walk
8	34–40	39–46	62–74	Fresh gale	Twigs break off trees
9	41–47	47–54	75–88	Strong gale	Branches break; slight damage to buildings
10	48–55	55–63	89–102	Whole gale	Trees are blown down; heavy damage to buildings
11	56–63	64–72	103–117	Storm	Widespread damage
12	64 and above	73 and above	118 and above	Hurricane	Extreme damage

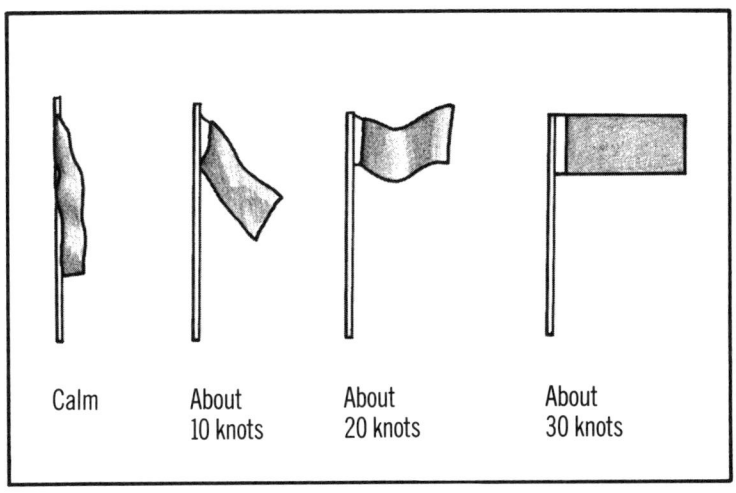

Figure 9. Estimating wind speed

wind recorded by an anemometer was 231 miles (370 km) per hour, or 200 knots, on April 12, 1934, on the top of Mount Washington, in New Hampshire. The speed of the winds in the jet stream may exceed 200 knots—230 miles (370 km) per hour.

You can make an anemometer for your weather station. Refer to Figure 10. You will need:

tape
2 plastic straws
a cap from a ballpoint pen
2 Ping-Pong balls
a crayon or marking pen
glue
*a piece of wire 10 inches (25 cm) long,
   made from a coat hanger*

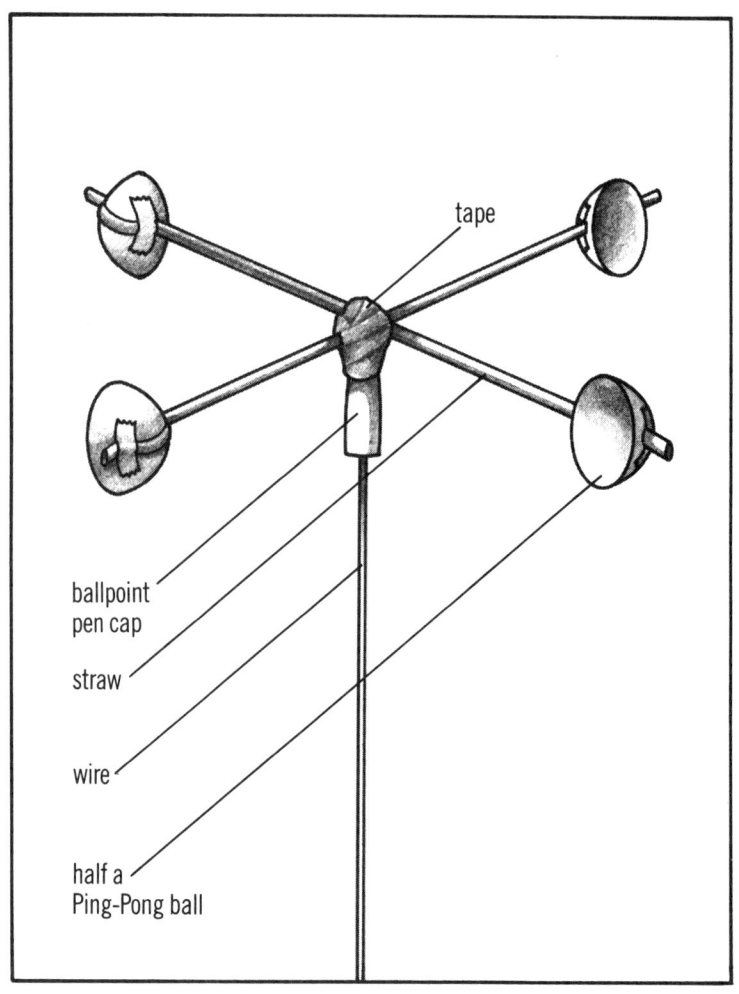

Figure 10. A demonstration anemometer

Use the tape to attach the two straws crossways to the tip of the pen cap. Cut each Ping-Pong ball in half. Color one of the halves. Glue one to each straw as close to the end as possible. Put the wire into the pen cap.

You can hold the anemometer in your hand, or you can attach it to a suitable object out in the open. To measure the wind speed, count the number of times the colored cup passes in front of you in a minute. This is a very crude measurement. If you want to include wind speed in your home-weather-station record, you can buy an inexpensive anemometer. Usually the instrument consists of both wind-direction and wind-speed indicators.

THE WIND-CHILL FACTOR • In Chapter Four, you found out that wind affects the rate of evaporation of sweat from the body. As the speed of the wind increases, the rate of evaporation increases, and also the transfer of heat is more rapid, causing the body to feel cooler. This is called the *wind-chill factor* and is often included in weather reports during winter. Everybody knows that cold and windy air feels worse than cold and calm air. But just how uncomfortable is the body? This depends on many things besides temperature and wind speed. It depends on how much and the type of clothing a person is wearing. It depends on whether it is a sunny or cloudy day. It depends on how a person's body senses cold.

Meteorologists have developed a formula that predicts how cold a person *may* feel at various temperatures and at various wind speeds. On a calm day when the temperature of the air is 10°F (-12°C), the body feels as if it is 10°F. But as the wind speed increases, the body feels as if the temperature has dropped. The chart on the following page shows how cold the body may feel at various wind speeds when the air temperature is 10°F.

Wind Speed in Miles per Hour	Sensed Temperature
5	7°F (−14°C)
10	−9°F (−23°C)
15	−18°F (−28°C)
20	−24°F (−31°C)
—	—
40	−36°F (−38°C)

CLOUDS • Since all weather factors are interrelated, winds can develop because of clouds, and clouds can be affected by wind. Clouds can cause changes in temperature by blocking out sunlight, which in turn can cause the formation of winds because of unequal heating of the earth's surface. And winds are involved in the creation of clouds by increasing the evaporation of water from the earth's surface.

Clouds are formed when moist warm air is slowly cooled until its relative humidity reaches 100%, its saturation point, and the water vapor in it condenses. This can happen when warm air slowly rises and cools or when warm air moves over a cooler surface, for example, when warm air from over a body of water moves over the cooler land. Sometimes, on a clear night, when the surface of the earth cools off rapidly, the moist air above it may cool below its saturation point and form a low cloud or fog. Fog is a cloud on the ground.

Meterologists name clouds by the way they are formed:

Cumulus clouds are formed by rising air currents. They are piled up and puffy. *Cumulus* means "piled up."

Stratus clouds are formed when a layer of air is cooled below its saturation point. These are sheets or layers. *Stratus* means "layered." Fog is a stratus cloud.

Above: Fair weather cumulus clouds
Below: Stratus clouds

Clouds are further classified by their heights:

High clouds are composed mainly of ice crystals, and their bases are about 20,000 feet (6,000 m) above the earth. They are generally thin and wispy.

Middle clouds usually have bases about 10,000 feet (3,000 m) above the ground.

Low clouds have bases that range from near the earth's surface to about 6,000 feet (1,800 m) up. They include *nimbostratus clouds*, which produce rain or snow, and

Nimbostratus clouds produce rain or snow.

cumulonimbus clouds—the thunderheads—whose bases seem almost to touch the ground and whose tops, carried by violent updrafts, may be as high as 75,000 feet (22,500 m). Tornadoes can be produced by such violent clouds.

You can observe the clouds and identify them by their shapes. You also can see in what direction they are traveling and whether they are moving quickly or slowly. You can record your cloud observations in your weather log. The National Weather Service has instruments which automatically measure the heights of clouds, their sizes from base to top, the directions of their movements, and the speeds at which they are moving, even at night.

SUGGESTED ACTIVITIES

1. Sometimes in the winter when people first try to start fires in their fireplaces, they have trouble. The smoke does not go up the chimney. Instead, it seeps out into the room. Can you think of at least two reasons why this may happen?

2. You can show that cold air is heavier than warm air. Use two cardboard or plastic containers of the same size and attach the same length of string to the bottom of each. Tie a short piece of string to the center of a ruler and hang the ruler in a doorway or from a table. Suspend an upside-down container from each end of the ruler. Balance them so that they hang at the same level.

Hold a lighted lamp at the mouth of one container. What happens as the air inside the container is heated? Remove the lamp and wait a few minutes. What happens? Now use the lamp to heat the air in the other container. What happens?

3. Some people find the direction of the wind by wetting a finger and holding it up. Explain how this works.

4. Evaluate the accuracy of your homemade anemometer by comparing the wind speed you determine using it with the wind speed registered on a commercial anemometer.

5. Estimate the wind speed by observing a flying flag. Compare your estimate with the speed recorded by an anemometer.

6. Correlate the presence of nimbostratus clouds with occurrence of a rainstorm or a snowstorm. Graph your observations, including the time elapsed between when you first sight the clouds and the first precipitation.

7. Graph the correlation between the presence of cumulonimbus clouds and the occurrences of thunderstorms.

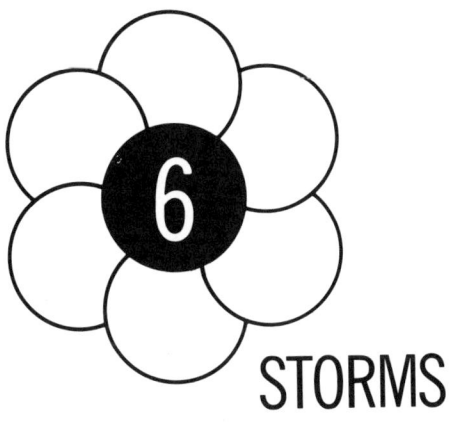

STORMS

The pilot of the round-the-world plane *Voyager* said, "I had acquired a healthy fear of weather." Such fear was not without reason. A violent storm could have torn his light airplane apart. A hurricane or tornado can destroy whole towns and cause great loss of life. A flash flood can wash out everything and everybody in its path. Because weather patterns deal with such large quantities of water and air, huge amounts of energy and destructive forces often are involved.

Large masses of air are constantly moving over the surface of the earth. An air mass can cover hundreds of thousands of square miles. But in all parts of such an air mass, the temperature and moisture conditions are practically the same. The air mass takes on and keeps the temperature and moisture conditions of the surface over which it forms. An air mass forming over the tropics is very warm, and an air mass forming over a polar region is very cold. An air mass forming over land is dry, while an air mass forming over the ocean is moist.

A mass of dry air exerts more pressure than a mass of moist air. An air mass with greater pressure is called a *high* or *anticyclone* and is shown on a weather map as an H. In the Northern Hemisphere, the motion of the air (the whirling winds) in a high is clockwise. The weather under a high is generally fair. A mass with less pressure is a *low*, or *cyclone*, and the winds in it whirl in a counterclockwise direction. It is shown on a map as an L. The weather under a low is generally cloudy with rain or snow. Figure 11 shows how wind circulates in anticyclones and cyclones.

When a hot, moist air mass collides with a cold, dry air mass, a weather *front* develops. The two air masses generally do not mix. If the cold air mass pushes the warm air mass back, it causes a cold front. If the cold air is pushed back by the warm air, a warm front is formed. If the boundary between the two air masses does not move, we have a stationary front. Wherever a front occurs, the weather is usually bad or stormy. After the front passes overhead, the weather clears. Figure 12 shows the symbols for various weather fronts on weather maps.

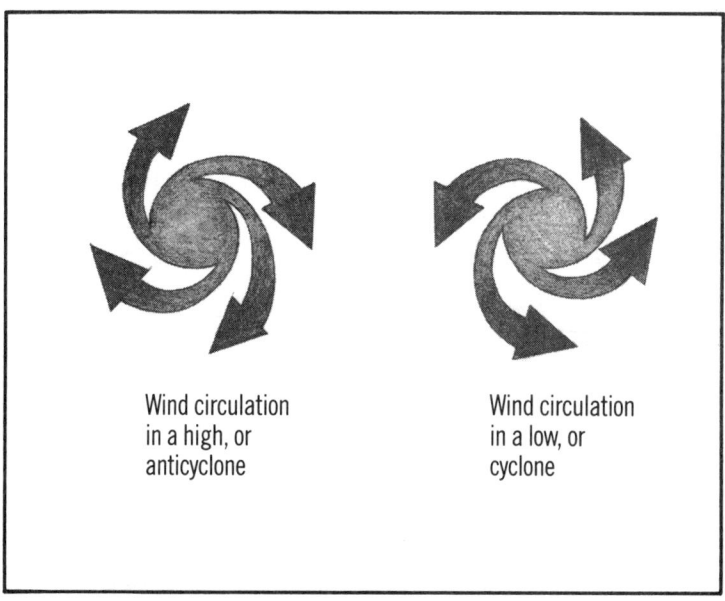

Figure 11. Wind circulation in anticyclones and cyclones

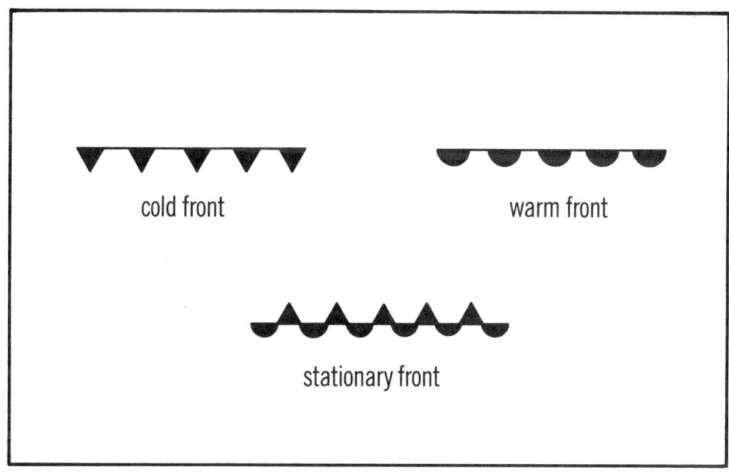

Figure 12. The symbols for fronts used on weather maps

HURRICANES • Some of the strongest storms on earth are called *hurricanes* when they occur in the Atlantic and *typhoons* in the Pacific. Hurricanes are tropical cyclones. They are lows that develop over ocean areas covered by warm, moist air masses. The average size of a hurricane is about 400 miles (640 km) across, and it has winds of at least 64 knots (74 miles—118 km—per hour) and sometimes over 130 knots (150 miles—240 km—per hour). Hurricanes are really giant whirlwinds in which the air moves in a large spiral around an *eye*, a calm center of extreme low pressure. Hurricanes begin as small tropical cyclones which usually drift slowly west-northwest (in the Northern Hemisphere), blown by the trade winds. As the storm moves farther from the equator, the forward speed increases to as much as 50 miles (80 km) per hour, and the eye can be as much as 40 miles (64 km) across and can take as long as four hours to pass overhead. The great storms are driven by the heat energy released by condensing water vapor and by the force of the prevailing winds. As a storm leaves the ocean and moves over land, it is starved for water and heat energy and generally falls apart.

Hurricanes in the Northern Hemisphere usually occur between June and October. On the average,

A satellite photo of Hurricane Gloria. Notice the whirlwind moving in a spiral around the eye.

there are six Atlantic hurricanes a year, but there were eleven hurricanes in 1916 and again in 1950. And in 1907 and 1914, there were no hurricanes at all. In 1950 and 1961, four hurricanes were blowing at the same time.

Even though the violent winds cause great damage, loss of life is usually due to drowning. The torrential rains fill the rivers and streams with too much water too quickly, and the water rushes out of its usual boundaries. Also, the storms cause surges of ocean water. Great domes of water, often 50 miles (80 km) wide, come sweeping across the coastline where the eye of the hurricane reaches land. Such a surge caused the death of more than seven thousand people in Galveston, Texas, on September 8, 1900, and destroyed over twenty-six hundred houses.

Because there are so few hurricanes each year, people often think, "It can't happen here." A man from Ohio who had just moved to Cape Cod, on the Massachusetts coast, ordered a barometer by mail. It arrived on September 21, 1938, and when he opened the package, the needle pointed to 27.8 inches, labeled HURRICANE. He was angry because he thought he had gotten a broken barometer. So he repacked it and carried it back to the post office on foot. On the way there it began to rain, and on the way home he really had to fight his way against the wind, sometimes crawling on his hands and knees. He finally made it, only to find that his house had been knocked down. The Great New England Hurricane had struck!

Some hurricanes can last for twelve hours or less,

but usually they continue for several days. Beginning in 1953, each hurricane was given a name. Hurricane Ginger wandered back and forth along the coasts of North Carolina and Virginia from September 5 to October 5, 1971, a total of thirty-one days.

TORNADOES • Another type of storm, a *tornado*, usually lasts only a few minutes and, compared to a hurricane, affects a relatively small area. But in that limited area it too can do tremendous damage. A tornado is a small but violently rotating column of air in contact with the ground. A *waterspout* is a tornado that touches down on water. The tornado is created during a thunderstorm when a funnel cloud dips down from the general cloud cover, gathering dust and debris as it whirls around.

Usually, more than 120 tornadoes strike the United States each year. Most of them touch down in the lower Mississippi Valley and Great Plains, although they have occurred in every state—even Hawaii. About two-thirds of them are "weak" and do little damage. About one-third are "strong"; these have wind speeds as much as 174 knots (200 miles—320 km—per hour), and touch down in a path up to 9 miles (14 km) long and 600 feet (180 m) wide. Only two out of every hundred tornadoes generally are "violent." Their wind speeds can reach 261 knots (300 miles—480 km—per hour), and their paths can be as much as 26 miles (41.6 km) long and 1 mile (1.6 km) wide. These rare tornadoes account for 70% of the yearly deaths and most of the property damage. The destruction is caused by a combination of the strong

A tornado is a violently rotating column
of air that causes enormous damage.

whirling winds and the impact of the debris they carry. For example, in 1975 a Mississippi tornado carried a home freezer for more than a mile. Imagine being hit by that!

Single tornadoes, such as the one that touched down in Saragosa, Texas on Friday, May 22, 1987, can demolish a whole town. Of the 350 people who lived there, 29 were killed and 120 were hurt. The tornado overturned the cars and trucks and leveled all the buildings. Sometimes a tornado can cross a very long strip. This happened on March 18, 1925, when the "Tri-State Tornado" traveled 219 miles across Missouri, Illinois, and Indiana. It lasted three and a half hours and killed 689 people. Sometimes tornadoes strike in groups. There was such a "super outbreak" of 148 tornadoes across thirteen states from the late afternoon of April 3 to the early morning of April 4, 1974. More than 300 people were killed and another 6,000 were injured, mainly by the flying debris.

Since tornadoes are generally local storms, they are not easy to forecast. The best instrument to detect a tornado funnel cloud is the human eye. You can become a volunteer sky watcher for Skywarn and provide the few minutes warning that can save lives. To join Skywarn, call or write your local Weather Service office or public safety agency.

THUNDERSTORMS • Tornadoes are born in thunderstorms. Although very few thunderstorms spawn tornadoes, all thunderstorms can be dangerous. Thunderstorms occur mainly in the late afternoon and early evening of the summer months when violent up-and-down movement of the air causes cumulonimbus clouds to form. These clouds—thunderheads—can extend upward more than 75,000 feet (22.5 km).

In the Midwest and the Northeast, such upward surges can be due to the heating of the air by the warm ground surface. These parts of the United States have an average of twenty to forty thunderstorms a year. In the Southeast, especially in Florida, the violent circulation is caused by the difference between land and water temperature. Eighty or ninety thunderstorms can occur there each year. There are few thunderstorms on the Pacific Coast, where the difference between land and water temperatures is small.

Air in turmoil can cause hail to form. *Hailstones* are raindrops that have frozen and become coated with more and more moisture as they are buffeted up and down in a cloud. When they finally fall to earth, they can be the size of a pea, or a golf ball, or a baseball, or a grapefruit. The largest hailstone ever measured was 17.5 inches (43.75 cm) around and weighed 1.7 pounds (765 g). It fell in Coffeyville, Kansas, on September 3, 1970.

The collision, rubbing together, and splitting of raindrops and ice crystals releases a tremendous

Thunderstorms can be dangerous. They occur primarily in the summer.

Most lightning—a "spark" of static electricity—does not hit the ground.

amount of energy in the form of static electricity—*lightning*. Lightning is an electric "spark" that jumps the gap from a part of a cloud that has a negative electric charge to another part of the same cloud or to another cloud that has a positive charge. Or it can jump from a cloud to the positively charged earth. Fewer than a third of the lightning strokes jump to the ground. A lightning discharge can be as great as 30,000,000 volts. Compare this with the 110 volts used to operate most household appliances.

The sudden tremendous heat from lightning causes sound waves in the surrounding air—*thunder*. Since light travels about 186,000 miles (300,000 km) per second, we see the lightning almost at the instant it happens. But sound travels at only 1,100 feet (330 m) per second, so it takes the thunder longer to reach our ears. That is why it seems as if the thunder follows the lightning.

The energy released by a thunderstorm can be greater than that of an atomic bomb, but it is not usable. A lightning stroke lasts less than a tenth of a second. Yet in that time, it can do tremendous damage. It can kill a person it strikes. It can knock out electrical devices such as generators and transformers. It can start fires. In a city or town such fires can often be put out before they cause much damage. But if lightning strikes in a forest, the fire it starts can burn for days or weeks and destroy everything in its path for hundreds of square miles. Every year in the United States, lightning kills about two hundred people and starts about seven thousand forest fires.

Lightning is attracted to anything that sticks up above the surrounding landscape—a tall tree, a pole, a person standing in an open field. The lightning travels down the object and into the ground. Benjamin Franklin, one of the first scientists to study lightning, encouraged people to put lightning rods on their houses. The rods have metal conductors leading into the ground. Lightning is attracted to the rod, which sticks up over the house, and travels down into the ground without damaging the house.

To protect yourself from lightning, avoid standing out in the open during a thunderstorm. If you can, take shelter in a house or in a closed automobile (not a convertible). Never stay in or near water or under a tall tree. If you cannot reach shelter, drop to your knees and bend forward and put your hands on your knees; DO NOT lie flat on the ground.

SUGGESTED ACTIVITIES

1. Sometimes during a hurricane, people think the storm is over and they go outdoors only to be caught in more storm. Why do they make such a mistake?

2. Practice reading the daily weather maps in the newspaper. Find the highs and lows. Find the cold fronts, warm fronts, and stationary fronts.

3. If there is a TV antenna on your house, why should it have a heavy wire leading from it into the ground?

4. If you are home when a tornado warning is broadcast, why should you take shelter in the basement or in a closet in the center of the house?

5. The sound of thunder travels 1 mile (1.6 km) every five seconds. The next time there is a thunderstorm, find out how far away it is. Use a watch with a second hand or say slowly "one thousand and one, one thousand and two, etc.," to count the seconds from the time you first see lightning to the moment when you hear thunder.

6. If you are caught outdoors during a thunderstorm, why should you never take shelter under a tall, isolated tree?

7. Prepare an illustrated exhibit of the "do's" and "don't's" of behavior during various types of storms.

8. You may have heard the expression: "It's too cold to snow." Use your thermometer to find out if there is any truth in the statement. On a day when you think it might snow—when there are nimbostratus clouds—record the temperature every hour, and especially when you see the first snowflake. Graph your observations. Compare the temperature pattern you find with the patterns of nonsnowy days just before and/or just after the snowfall.

9. There are many different kinds of snow. The Eskimos, for example, have more than forty names for various types of snow. Ski reports describe the condition of a slope according to its snowcover: loose, packed, wet, dry, powdery, etc. But the flakes, as they fall, usually are hexagonal, although even in the same snowfall they vary in design. If you live in the snowbelt, collect snowflakes on a piece of cold black plastic or cloth. Use a magnifying glass to examine them. Draw the various designs you find.

One or two days after the snowfall, use a magnifying glass to examine samples of the snow on the ground. Can you see any hexagonal crystals? Draw what you see.

10. When it hails, collect a few hailstones. Place them on a cold metal or plastic plate. Cut them open and observe how they were formed. Are they all the same? Draw what you see.

7
RECORDING AND PREDICTING THE WEATHER

People have recorded the weather in America almost since the first Europeans settled here. As early as 1644, the Reverend John Campanius Holm, who lived near what is now Wilmington, Delaware, kept a daily record of weather conditions. So did many others in the American colonies, including George Washington and Thomas Jefferson. But they did not try to predict the weather even a day or two ahead.

Benjamin Franklin was the first weather forecaster in America even though his information was usually several days old and he had few instruments to help him. Since his time, the gathering of weather information from all over the world has become almost instantaneous, and more and better instruments have been developed. Today, we can generally rely on the forecasts issued by the National Weather Service.

For about a hundred years after Franklin, there were many attempts to gather weather information. During the War of 1812 and for about forty years afterward, one duty of the surgeons in the U.S. Army hospitals was to observe the weather and keep records. The surgeons were given the task because doctors believed that the weather influenced people's health.

Later, in 1849, Joseph Henry, the first secretary and director of the Smithsonian Institution in Washington, D.C., set up a large network of weather observers. He sent weather instruments all across the country to about five hundred operators of the newly invented telegraph system. The volunteers, now called cooperative weather observers, made their observations at the same times each day, and telegraphed them to Washington. There, Henry drew maps of the reported weather conditions and often made predictions based on them. These predictions were the first published weather forecasts in the United States.

Joseph Henry's network became part of the National Weather Service, which was first named the Weather Bureau. The Weather Service was created by law in 1870, and for twenty years it was part of the Signal Service of the U.S. Army. Then it moved to the Department of Agriculture. This was a logical move at that time since farmers were the group most concerned with changes in weather, especially unseasonable frosts.

The Weather Service was moved again in 1940, this time to the Department of Commerce because of the needs of the growing air transportation industry. Today, it is still in the Department of Commerce as part of the National Oceanic and Atmospheric Administration—NOAA. NOAA is where the National Weather Service belongs because, as you have learned, weather depends on the general oceanic and atmospheric conditions.

The National Weather Service gathers information from all across the United States, from all across the world, from deep in the oceans, and from thousands of feet up in the atmosphere. There are more than four hundred weather stations employing some five thousand people. Thousands of observations are made daily by these government workers and by volunteers across the land, by sailors on ships at sea, by aviators in airplanes, by radar, by instruments in balloons, ocean buoys, and earth-orbiting satellites.

These sources report the temperatures and barometric pressure of the air at various heights, the temperatures of the water at various depths, the amount of sunshine, the moisture content of the air, the cloud formations, the wind speeds and directions on the surface and in the upper atmosphere, the locations and movements of air masses, the path of the

jet stream, the courses of ocean currents, the amounts of pollution in the air, the amounts of rainfall and snowfall, and the water levels of lakes, streams, and rivers.

Most of this information is sent automatically by the instruments, usually by radio, to central stations where it is entered into computers. The computers can store and process the data. The computers are programmed so that a meteorologist can retrieve any information needed, for example, the temperatures for a given location over the past forty-eight hours. Complicated formulas also have been programmed into the computers to use the information collected to predict the weather. These predictions can be for a particular place or for a whole region, for the next day or for the next week or the next month. All the meteorologist has to do is type the request and the computer prints out the forecast and even draws a weather map. The picture on page 96 shows a meteorologist using a computer in a weather station. Notice the map on one screen.

The National Weather Service—a part of the National Oceanic and Atmosphere Administration—collects and disseminates weather information. This meteorological satellite—operated by NOAA—keeps a weather eye on the Earth's cloud cover to improve weather forecasting and to gather data on climatic changes.

Forecasters provide nearly two million predictions per year to the public and commercial interests.

The job of the Weather Service is what its name implies: to serve the needs of the people. It is not enough to gather the information; the information must reach the people who need to know. People need to know the weather for the next day, and they need to be warned about emergencies: blizzards, tornadoes, hurricanes, severe thunderstorms, floods, *tsunamis*, unusual air pollution. To do this, the Weather Service uses direct teletypewriter service to many local TV and radio stations, its own NOAA Weather Radio, telephone company "Weather-by-Phone" hookups, and cable TV weather channels. It issues more than two million forecasts and warnings each year. It also provides the information on which private companies such as Accu-Weather base their forecasts.

Accu-Weather was founded by a professor of meteorology at Pennsylvania State University. His organization uses Weather Service information to predict changes and alert their special customers. For example, some school districts rely on Accu-Weather to tell them when schools should be closed because of heavy snowfalls. The Philadelphia International Airport wants dense fog warnings to keep the runways safe. The Port of Galveston, Texas, needs special hurricane warnings to prevent damage to shipping. Accu-Weather also provides forecasts for many radio and TV stations and for newspapers. Private companies cater to the particular needs of each customer, while the Weather Service serves the general public.

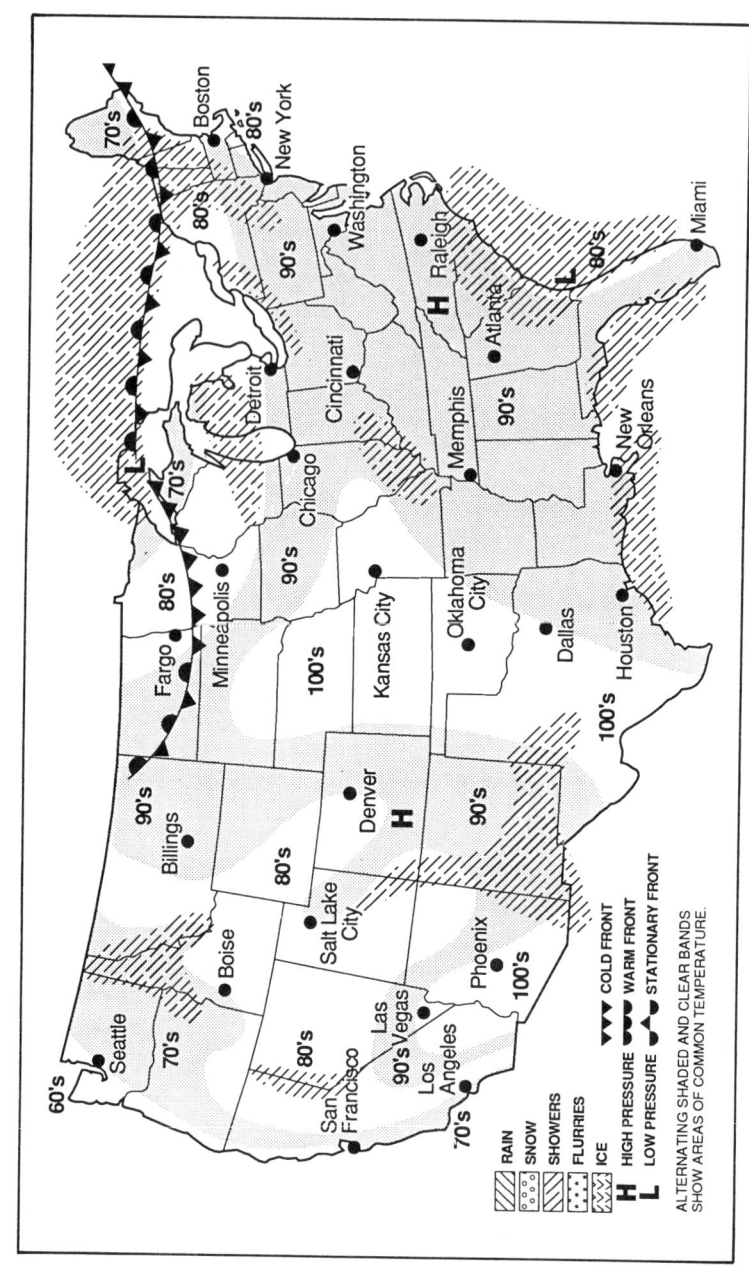

A daily weather map from a newspaper

Some newspapers use the Weather Service's daily maps; some use maps issued by private companies. Weather maps are easy to read. Notice the different kinds of fronts that appear on the weather map photo. Can you find the lows and the highs?

If you collect weather maps from the newspaper for three or four days in a row, you can see the movements of fronts and weather patterns across the country. After three days, try to predict the weather for the next day for your hometown. Unless the pattern stalls, you should be able to forecast whether it will be fair or stormy.

The Weather Service does not use volunteers to prepare forecasts, but they still use some eleven thousand cooperative observers to help gather information on temperature and precipitation. If, after you have recorded the weather in your home weather station regularly for several months, you think you would like to become a cooperative observer, you can contact your local Weather Service office. But remember—a volunteer must record the weather *every* day of the year!

SUGGESTED ACTIVITIES

1. Setting up your home weather station:

Location. To ensure a truer recording of the weather factors, place the instruments out in the open away from buildings, trees, and other obstructions. All instruments should be close together for convenience in observing. Assemble the instruments far enough apart so that they do not interfere with each other. For example, the wind vane and/or anemometer must have enough space to turn freely.

The barometer and thermometer should be protected from the rain. Any cover you put over them should be well slotted so that sufficient air reaches the instruments for them to record the actual conditions of the atmosphere. The sling psychrometer can be stored when not in use.

You can make a simple housing for your instruments from a wooden box without a top. Place the box on its side with the open top facing you. Make a slotted door for the opening out of strips of wood or slats from a venetian blind. The slats should be angled down so that rain will not drip into the box. You can waterproof the rest of the box by sealing any cracks with putty. Use a waterproof paint to complete the construction.

Recording. Make copies of the chart shown on page 101. Keep the charts in a looseleaf notebook or sturdy binder. Record your observations as you make them.

2. If you have access to a computer, you can enter your daily observations.

Use the computer to compile such statistical information as:

- monthly and/or yearly temperature graph
- monthly and/or yearly precipitation graph

Use the computer to retrieve such information as:

- lowest temperature of the month or year

HOME-WEATHER-STATION DAILY RECORD

Observer _____
Location _____

Date	Time	Barometric pressure	Temperature	Relative humidity	Rainfall (snowfall)	Wind direction	Wind speed	Cloud condition

- highest temperature of the month or year
- greatest precipitation of the month or year
- highest wind speed of the month or year
- highest relative humidity of the month or year
- lowest relative humidity of the month or year
- lowest barometric pressure of the month or year
- highest barometric pressure of the month or year
- number of days of the month or year without any precipitation
- number of days of the month or year when the temperature fell below freezing

3. Use the computer to print out your forecast for the next day. Distribute your forecast to your classmates or post it on a bulletin board.

4. Keep an account of how accurate your forecasts are. Compare your forecasts with those in the daily newspaper, the *Farmer's Almanac*, the televised and radio-broadcast forecasts.

5. If your school has a closed-circuit television system or public address system, ask if you may present your weather forecast each day.

6. Use your recorded weather observations to determine whether there is any truth in such weather folklore as:

- Red sky at night, sailors' delight (fair weather).

- Red sky in the morning, sailors take warning (foul weather).
- A ring around the moon means rain.
- If the groundhog sees its shadow on February 2 (Groundhog Day), there will be six more weeks of winter.

WEATHER INSTRUMENT SUPPLIERS

Edmund Scientific
101 E. Gloucester Pike
Barrington, NJ 08007

H & R Corporation
401 E. Erie Ave.
Philadelphia, PA 19134

Radio Shack
One Tandy Center
Fort Worth, TX 76102

Taylor Scientific Instrument
95 Glenn Bridge Road
Arden, NC 28704

Wind and Weather
P.O. Box 1012-W
Mendocino, CA 95460

Local hardware or housewares stores

GLOSSARY

Acid rain—rain that contains sulfuric acid.
Anemometer—an instrument for measuring wind speed.
Aneroid—without liquid.
Anticyclone—an air mass with greater than normal pressure.
Atmosphere—the layer of air (gases) surrounding the earth.
Atmospheric pressure—the weight (push) of a column of air; it is measured in inches or centimeters.
Barometer—an instrument for measuring atmospheric pressure.
Calibrate—to devise a scale for an instrument.
Climate—the average weather for an area.
Cyclone—an air mass with less than normal pressure.
Eye—the hurricane's calm center with extreme low pressure.
Front—the boundary between two air masses.
Hailstone—ice formed around a frozen raindrop.

High—an air mass with greater than normal pressure; an anticyclone.
Hurricane—a tropical cyclone in the Atlantic.
Hygrometer—an instrument for measuring atmospheric humidity.
Jet stream—a tubelike belt of fierce winds in the upper atmosphere.
Lightning—a "spark" of static electricity.
Low—an air mass with less than normal pressure; a cyclone.
Meteorologist—a weather scientist.
Relative humidity—amount of moisture in the air.
Saturation point—the point at which the air can hold no more moisture; 100% humidity.
Sling psychrometer—an instrument for measuring relative humidity.
Temperature—degree of hotness or coldness.
Thermometer—an instrument for measuring temperature.
Thunder—the sound produced when a bolt of lightning heats the surrounding air.
Tornado—a violently rotating column of air.
Tsunami—a huge, deadly ocean wave caused by an earthquake.
Typhoon—a tropical cyclone in the Pacific.
Vacuum—an empty space; a space from which air has been removed.
Waterspout—a tornado that touches down on water.
Weather—the condition of the atmosphere for short periods of time.
Wind-chill factor—the lower temperature a body senses because of increased wind speed.
Wind vane—an instrument to show the direction in which the wind is blowing.

BIBLIOGRAPHY

Allen, Oliver E. *Atmosphere*. New York: Time-Life Books, 1983.

Alth, Max. *Disastrous Hurricanes and Tornadoes*. New York: Franklin Watts, 1981.

Cohen, Daniel. *What's Happening to Our Weather*. New York: M. Evans & Co., 1979.

Dunlop, S. *The Larousse Guide to Weather Forecasting*. New York: Larousse, 1982.

Fradin, Dennis Brindell. *Blizzards and Winter Weather*. Chicago: Children's Press, 1983.

———. *Droughts*. Chicago: Children's Press, 1983.

Gallant, Roy A. *Earth's Changing Climate*. New York: Four Winds, 1979.

Heuer, Kenneth. *Rainbows, Halos, and Other Wonders: Light and Color in the Atmosphere.* New York: Dodd, Mead, 1978.

Lambert, David. *Weather and Its Works.* New York: Facts on File, 1984.

———. *The Work of the Wind.* New York: Bookwright Press, 1984.

Lye, Keith. *Weather and Climate.* Lexington, MA: Silver, Burdett, 1984.

Purvis, George. *Weather and Climate.* New York: Bookwright Press, 1984.

Sattler, Helen R. *Nature's Weather Forecasters.* New York: Elsevier/Nelson, 1978.

Stommel, Henry. *Volcano Weather: The Story of 1816, the Year Without a Summer.* New York: Seven Seas Press, 1983.

Williams, Terry Tempest. *The Secret Language of Snow.* San Francisco: Sierra Club Books, 1984.

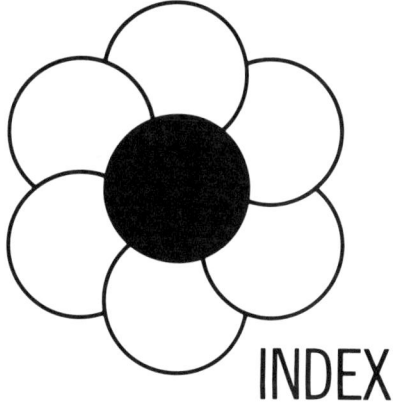

INDEX

Italic page numbers indicate illustrative figures.

Accu-Weather, 97
Acid rain, 55–58, *56*, 105
Air pollution, 97
Air pressure. *See* Atmospheric pressure
Altimeter, 30
Anaximenes, 19
Anemometer, 16, *68*, 74, 100, 105; assembly instructions for, 67–69; definition/explanation of, 85–87
Aneroid, 105
Aneroid barometer, 25–29, *26*
Aneroid thermometer, 41–42
Anticyclone, 76, 77, 105
Atmosphere, 18–19, 32–34, 105
Atmospheric pressure, 19–22, *21*, *23*, 29, 30, 41, 105; and barometers, 22–25; experimentation of, 20–22

Barometer, 15, 16, *23*, 41, 100, 105; assembly instructions for (aneroid), 25–29; and atmospheric pressure, 22–25; definition/explanation of, 22–23; a mercury, 23–25; suggested activities for, 29–31
Barometric pressure, 30, 31, 93, 102
Beaufort, Francis, 65
Beaufort Scale, 66
Boiling point of water, 41
Boyle, Robert, 15

Calibration, 24, 30, 42, 43, 105
Celsius, Anders, 41
Climate, 12, 105
Clouds, 70–74, 84, 89. *See also* name of specific cloud
Cold front, 76, 88
Cumulonimbus clouds, 73, 74, 84
Cumulus clouds, 71, *71*
Cyclone, 76, 77, 105

Eye (hurricane), *77*, 78, 105

Fahrenheit, Gabriel, 15, 41
Flood, 75, 97
Fog, 70, 71
Forecasting, *96*; history of, 12–15, 91–93; suggested activities for, 99–103
Franklin, Benjamin, 12–15, *14*, 88, 91–92
Freezing point of water, 41
Front, 76, 77, 88, 99, 105. *See also* specific type of front
Frost, 10
Funnel cloud (tornado), 83

Hailstones, 45, 84, 90, 105
Heat transference, 38–40

Henry, Joseph, 92
High (air pressure), 76, 88, 106
High clouds, 72
Home weather station, 16–17, 99–103
Hurricane, 75, 77, 78–81, 85, 88, 97, 106
Hygrometer, 48, 54, 106

Ice, 10
Instrument suppliers, 104

Jet stream, 64–65, 95, 106

Knot (wind speed), 85

Lightning, *86*, 87–88, 106
Low (air pressure), 76, 78, 88, 106
Low clouds, 72

Mercury barometer, 15, 23–25
Meteorological satellite, *94*
Meteorologist, 10, 16, 106
Middle clouds, 72
Moisture experimentation, 44–46

National Oceanic and Atmospheric Administration, *94*
National Weather Service, 16, 50, 73, 85, 92, 93, *94*, 97, 99
Newton, Isaac, 15
Nimbostratus clouds, 72, *72*, 74, 89
NOAA (Natioal Oceanic and Atmospheric Administration), 93, 97

Precipitation, 50–52, 102; suggested activities for, 53–54. *See also* Rain/snow; Hail; Sleet

110

Prediction. *See* Forecasting

Rain/snow, 45, 50, 51–52, 72, *72*, 76, 95
Rain/snow gauge, 16, 52, 53
Relative humidity, *48*, 53, 54, 70, 102, 106; definition/explanation of, 46–47; measurement of, 48–50

Saturation point, 47, 70, 71, 106
Skywarn, 83
Sleet, 10, 45
Sling psychrometer, 16, 48, *48*, 50, 53, 100, 106
Snow, 10, *37*, 89
Stationary front, 76, 88
Storms, 88–90. *See also* specific type of storm
Stratus clouds, 71, *71*
Sulfuric acid, *56*, 58

Tambora volcano, 35, *36*
Temperature, 102, 106; definition/explanation of, 32; and hot vs. cold air, 32–39, 43
Thermometer, 15, 16, *39*, 100, 106; an aneroid, 41–42; assembly instructions for, 38–40; definition/explanation of, 40; history of, 41–42; suggested activities for, 42–43
Thunder, 87, 89, 106

Thunderstorm, 74, 83–88, *85*, 89, 97
Tornado, 75, 81–83, *82*, 88, 97, 106
Torricelli, Evangelista, 15, 23–25
Trade winds, 78
Tsunami, 97, 106
Typhoon, 78, 106

Vacuum, 24, 106
Vidie, Lucien, 25
Voyager, *8*, 9–10, *11*, 75

Warm front, 76, 88
Water cycle, 45–46, *46*
Waterspout (tornado), 81, 106
Water vapor, 45, 70
Weather, 12, 106
Weather Bureau, 92–93
Weather instrument suppliers, 104
Weather map, *79*, 88, *98*, 99
Wet-bulb thermometer, 48
Wind: direction of, *63*; experimentation with, 58–59; measurement of, 66, 67–69; patterns of, 59–60, *60*; speed of, *67*, 74, *85*, 102; suggested activities for, 73–74
Wind-chill factor, 69–70, 106
Wind vane, 16, 60–64, *62*, *63*, 100, 106

ABOUT THE AUTHORS

Beulah and Harold Tannenbaum have written many children's books and materials for textbooks on various aspects of science, including weather. Mr. Tannenbaum is a retired teacher; Mrs. Tannenbaum was a children's librarian and science consultant.

The Tannenbaums live in Pennsylvania.